SOMERSET
COUNTY CRICKET
SCRAPBOOK

287

A.Thompson

SOMERSET
COUNTY CRICKET
SCRAPBOOK

VIC MARKS
Foreword by Ian Botham

**PICTORIAL
PRESENTATIONS**

SOUVENIR PRESS

First published 1984 by Souvenir Press Ltd,
43 Great Russell Street, London WC1B 3PA
and simultaneously in Canada

ISBN 0 285 62632 9 casebound
ISBN 0 285 62631 0 paperback

Typeset by CCC, printed and bound in Great Britain by
William Clowes Limited, Beccles and London

I should like to express my thanks to the following:
In Taunton—
Eric Coombes and the *Somerset County Gazette* for permission to reproduce their photographs and various quotations from their columns.
Eric Hill for recalling the old days.
Jock McCombe for his photographs and his continuous praise.
Mike Taylor for his valiant attempts to organise me.
Doris.
My colleagues at Somerset for helping me remember what happened.
In Tiverton—
Sally Patrick for her immaculate typing and constant encouragement.
My wife for her criticisms (valid, as usual) with apologies for ignoring most of them.

I am also grateful to the following for permission to reproduce copyright material: Bodley Head Ltd. for a quotation from *46 Not Out* by R. C. Robertson-Glasgow, published by Hollis & Carter; Redcliffe Press Ltd., for the extract from *From Grace to Botham* by David Foot; Macdonald & Co (Publishers) Ltd. for quotations from *The Hand that Bowled Bradman* by Bill Andrews, *I Don't Bruise Easily* by Brian Close and *Wisden Cricketers' Almanack 1978*; Sporting Handbooks Ltd. for quotations from *Wisden Cricketers' Almanack* 1968 and 1973; George Allen & Unwin for five extracts from *Slices of Cricket* by Peter Roebuck; Pelham Books Ltd. for a quotation from *My Incredible Innings* by Bill Alley; World's Work Ltd. for three quotations from *Viv Richards* by Vivian Richards with David Foot; Times Newspapers for a quotation from John Woodcock's article in *The Times* of 2nd September, 1978; Somerset County Cricket Club for an extract from the article by Eric Hill in their 1983 *Handbook*; Mr John Arlott for his comments taken from Mervyn Kitchen's benefit brochure and Mr Alan Gibson for a quotation from Peter Denning's benefit brochure; Mr John Davies for quotations from *Up From Somerset for the Cup*; S & G Press Agency for the photographs on pages 7, 28 and 32; Central Press Photos for the photographs on pages 10 and 12 (bottom).

CONTENTS

FOREWORD

I remember walking into the county ground at Taunton one damp, chilly morning in April, 1974, as a wide-eyed and excited newcomer. Like the other new boys that morning, I did not quite know what to expect around the next corner. It was a time of discovery. Somerset were neither fashionable nor successful at that time, yet with my built-in optimism allied to the innocence of youth, I figured that things were about to change for the better. Being unfashionable has never bothered me, but being unsuccessful has always been painful.

Two of my fellow apprentices reporting for duty that day were Vic Marks and one Vivian Richards, and none of us could have guessed that, ten years later, we would be looking back on a decade of glorious achievement – the ten years, in fact, during which the Cinderella county finally made it to the ball.

Now my colleague Vic Marks, who has played a key part in Somerset's dramatic rise, is able to tell the full, riveting, rags-to-Richards story. It is a delight to turn back the pages of Somerset's history and meet characters like the Rev. Stirling Cookesley Voules, R. C. Robertson-Glasgow, Sammy Woods and Jack White, the farmer from Stogumber. The names, the dramas, the great deeds, are all recorded; the tragedies have been researched along with the triumphs.

For much of the time, it has been a case of 'so near yet so far': Brian Close, so near to winning a trophy but finally missing out in a bizarre last match before retirement; Somerset, so near to their first-ever trophy before losing the crucial John Player League game against Glamorgan in 1976; and so near to a Gillette Cup and Sunday League double in 1978 before losing in one, nightmare weekend.

Yet the disappointments served to increase our appetite to bring a trophy back to Taunton, and when the major prizes started to arrive we believed they were reward for a Somerset effort that stretched back to the early 1970s.

As this book points out, however, the battle continues. While the one-day successes have been marvellous for the county and its supporters, the championship must remain our top priority. That, hopefully, is another story . . .

Ian Botham

INTRODUCTION: THE FIRST NINETY YEARS

Somerset cricket over its first ninety years is noted for its unpredictability, its collection of larger-than-life characters from such contrasting parts of the globe as Sydney and Georgetown, Watchet and Stogumber, and its complete lack of success. Throughout this period the headquarters at Taunton was rarely deserted and its spectators were seldom disappointed. The ground's ideal situation in the centre of town, with the market and railway station just a firm, straight drive away, coupled with its homely, rural atmosphere, ensured that visiting holidaymakers as well as local farmers could not resist popping in for a few hours. The short boundaries and true pitch rarely failed to produce a feast of runs (especially if the opposition was batting), and its intimacy enabled the visitor to catch the smiles and grimaces of his heroes out in the middle.

Supporting Somerset was a worthwhile occupation unless your yardstick was simply a succession of Somerset victories and the prospect of a Championship title: but not many followers dared to hope for such extravagances. Their highest expectation was to see the giants of Yorkshire and Surrey just occasionally humbled by the locals. If not, they would be satisfied with annual glimpses of the masters, from Grace to May, displaying their skills. A brief statistical survey suggests that this approach was the only realistic one to adopt. Below I list the sum total of Somerset's success in the County Championship up until 1965.

In 1892	Somerset finish		3rd	under	H. T. Hewett
„ 1919	„	„	5th	„	John Daniell
„ 1946	„	„	4th	„	E. F. Longrigg
„ 1958	„	„	3rd	„	Maurice Tremlett
„ 1963	„	„	3rd	„	Harold Stephenson

It is hardly an awe-inspiring record. Demonstrating Somerset's less successful eras is much easier. From 1952 to 1955 the club finished bottom, a position they have occupied ten times in their history. During that period they won ten matches out of 112. Nonetheless there were plenty of excellent cricketers and exciting matches to cherish during these ninety years, when Somerset's reputation for occasional brilliance coupled with disastrous failure was born.

Harold Stephenson, good enough to tour as Godfrey Evans' deputy. (S & G Press Agency).

It is typical of Somerset's haphazard early history that the club should have been formed at a meeting in Devon after a match at Sidmouth on 18th August, 1875. Four resolutions were passed:

1 There shall be no county ground.
2 The club shall depend on support by voluntary contributions.
3 County matches shall be played on any ground in the county that may be selected by the Committee.
4. A president, vice-president, treasurer and secretary by nomination and a committee of nine gentlemen, three from each division of the county, shall be appointed.

Of course, there have been many changes since then: the county ground was acquired in 1886 and for better or worse the size of the committee has mushroomed. But the tradition of playing county cricket almost anywhere was maintained until very recently. As well as the established centres at Taunton, Bath and Weston, the towns of Frome, Yeovil, Glastonbury, Wells and Street have welcomed some of the legendary figures of the game.

With considerable pride I inform you that the first Somerset captain, the Reverend Stirling Cookesley Voules, was born less than 100 yards from my own birthplace, in the vicarage at Middle Chinnock, near Crewkerne. I spent hours of my youth striking fours (ie. hitting the ball beyond the coalshed door) in the vicar's back yard. I'd like to think that the young Stirling did the same before settling down to the weightier matters of graduation at Oxford and ordination.

There were several historic moments for spectators to savour at the county ground after Somerset's official entry into the Championship in 1891. The following year the captain H. T. Hewett and L. C. H. Palairet, all grace and artistry, added 346 for the first wicket against Yorkshire – a record that's rarely been threatened. In 1895 A. C. Maclaren of Lancashire hit 424 in 470 minutes out of a total of 801, the highest individual score ever made in England. In the same year W.G. chose Taunton as the venue for his hundredth hundred: the event was celebrated by champagne which so revitalised the doctor that he proceeded to make 288 in 320 minutes.

Coincidentally it was also at Taunton in 1925 that Jack Hobbs scored his 126th century, thus surpassing Grace's record. R. C. Robertson-Glasgow was bowling for Somerset on this occasion and in his delightful autobiography *Forty-six Not Out*[1] he recorded the scene on the Monday morning as Hobbs resumed his innings, 91 not out:

It must have been a long weekend for Hobbs. Even at Sunday afternoon tea he was nailed by the motion picture photographers. On Monday morning the crowd poured in again and Somerset committee men beamed affably alike on friends, enemies and total strangers. Jim Bridges had the first over at Hobbs, whose partner, worthily, was Douglas Jardine. Hobbs scored three singles and so was 94 when I took up the attack. How I longed to unloose something supremely and eternally unplayable, an inswinger, say, pitching on the leg stump and sending the middle flying. Never the time and the place and the 'snifter' all together! I bowled four running that were very straight and proper. He played back to each one and I chose to believe that he was nearly late on the fourth. Then, Lord bless me, I bowled a no ball. Whack went she to the square leg boundary. From the sixth and last ball he scored a single: 99. Then with a single to leg off Bridges, he was there. At last the cheering died away and, at the end of the over, all on the field shook him by the hand. Percy Fender, the Surrey captain, carried out a glass. Hobbs ever since has maintained that it contained only ginger ale. Be that as it may, he raised the glass, and in the handsome words of a chronicler 'bowed to the crowd before partaking of the refreshment'. Within a few minutes he was caught at the wicket for 101.

Robertson-Glasgow qualifies as the most literate cricketer to have played for Somerset, although his position is presently being challenged by Peter Roebuck.

Enough of the visitors. Let's dwell on a few of our own heroes, though their birthplaces will not be confined to the boundaries of Somerset.

Initially Somerset relied heavily on two contrasting all rounders, Len Braund and Sammy Woods. Braund's quick leg breaks and sound batting were surprisingly rejected by Surrey but avidly snapped up by Somerset, where he performed with such distinction that he won 23 caps for England. His contributions were decisive in creating Somerset's reputation as a 'Team of Surprises'. From 1900 to 1902 Yorkshire won three Championships losing only two matches, both to Somerset. The most famous was at Leeds in 1901 when Somerset were dismissed in the first innings for 87. Yorkshire replied with 325, whereupon Palairet and Braund followed up their first innings noughts with hundreds in the second as Somerset totalled 630. Not even the Yorkshiremen could recover from such a turnabout and Braund and B. Cranfield, his spin partner, bowled them out for

Peter Wight hits out during his century against the 1953 Australian tourists. (Somerset County Gazette).

Harold Gimblett, Somerset's greatest home grown batsman. (Somerset County Gazette).

Jack Meyer, Captain in 1947, too busy in India and at Millfield to play regularly for the county. (Somerset County Gazette).

130, producing a remarkable triumph by 279 runs, a result no doubt causing spilt milk at breakfast tables in both Yorkshire and Somerset.

For all Braund's excellence, I've no doubt that S. M. J. Woods was the crowd's favourite; he'd probably shared a drink with most of them at some time in his life. Born in Sydney, he had the rare distinction of having played for both England and Australia. He played for the county for twenty years (1891–1910), captaining the side for twelve, as a tireless fast bowler, strong hitter and, as David Foot has written[2], 'the most gregarious sportsman of his day'. He quickly adopted the West Country as his home and often astounded companions whilst hunting on the Quantocks by producing bottles of ale from underneath certain bushes. He always took the precaution of storing away these vital supplies for future emergencies.

David Foot again[2]: 'If there was something on in Taunton, he was there. When the Fair arrived he climbed roguishly in the ring. He skittled with rosy-faced zeal and sang very acceptably in tune at the village harvest homes. He was extrovert, noisy and offended no one.' I've a sneaking suspicion that Ian Botham would have enjoyed sharing a dressing-room with Sammy Woods, for they appear to have much in common. Maybe Ian will be considered the greater cricketer, but Woods was certainly the superior singer.

After the First World War the team relied upon a band of amateurs enlisted by their authoritarian captain John Daniell, himself a Cambridge blue and an English rugby international. Of the successful 1919 side J. C. W. MacBryan, R. C. Robertson-Glasgow, M. D. Lyon and J. C. White all played for the gentlemen in the prestigious fixture against the players. Daniell contrived to stretch the birth qualification rules for county cricketers to its limits. When he approached the New Zealander T. C. Lowry about playing for Somerset he was told that his birthplace was Wellington. Since there is a town of that name just seven miles from the county ground, Daniell is said to have closed the deal to the satisfaction of the MCC. Future exchanges with Lord's were to prove more complex.

Somerset's bowling during this period depended chiefly upon a phlegmatic farmer from Stogumber, Jack White, of whom Robertson-Glasgow once said, 'Whether it was cows or batsmen he had the treatment for the trouble.' He was an unusual slow left arm bowler because he relied very little upon spin; varied flight and sustained accuracy brought him well over 2,000 first class wickets and fifteen caps for England. He was one of the outstanding successes on the

Eric Hill opened with Gimblett after the war and captained Somerset's first XI side. Now a respected journalist. (Central Press Photos).

triumphant tour of Australia in 1928/9 when, at the age of 37, in the Fourth Test at Adelaide he bowled 124 overs and took 13 wickets for 256. On his return to England the locals dragged his car with ropes back to his home in Combe Florey and a spontaneous fund raised £1,000 for him. No doubt the celebrations brought a rare smile to the face of this imperturbable Somerset farmer. His 28 years of yeoman service to the club made him the county's most prolific wicket taker, a record which is unlikely to be surpassed.

The amateurs were gradually augmented by a stout group of professionals, all now part of Somerset cricket folklore. For 25 years (1924–49) Wally Luckes stood behind the stumps, reliable and self-effacing, not dissimilar in style to Trevor Gard (I imagine). Horace Hazell (1929–52), a rotund and endearing cricketer from North Somerset, was White's stand-by and subsequent replacement. He was remarkably economical: in 1949 against Gloucestershire he

Horace Hazell (1929–52) finding his length in the nets. (Somerset CCC).

bowled 17 consecutive overs without conceding a run. More diverting was his comical yet surprisingly effective batting at number 11. From a solicitor's office in Bath came Bertie Buse (1929–53) 'all bat and bum', one of cricket's rarities – a batsman who could defend painstakingly all day and still warm the hearts of the crowd. His inswingers were more dangerous than they appeared, as the Indian tourists discovered in 1946 when in harness with Andrews he bowled them out for 64 before lunch. He was a popular cricketer and no doubt kept smiling even when his benefit match at Bath in 1953 was completed at tea time on the first day.

The schoolboys' favourites were the two strapping opening bowlers Arthur Wellard (1927–50) and Bill Andrews (1930–47). Wellard's batting was the bane of auctioneers at Taunton market. When he was at the wicket prospective buyers drifted over the road in search of greater excitement. Twice he hit five sixes in an over; one of the occasions was when Somerset completed a remarkable double against the 1936 Champions, Derbyshire. At Wells Wellard took nine wickets in the match and, when all appeared lost, hit seven sixes and eight fours, making 86 out of 102 in under an hour for a famous one-wicket victory. Of the 12,000 runs he scored in first class cricket 3,000 were from six-hits – a ratio that not even Ian Botham can match. However his main role was as a fast away swing bowler, who later also became an accomplished off spinner. He captured well over 1,500 wickets for Somerset, which places him second to White in the record books.

His partner Bill Andrews became an integral part of the club for almost fifty years. He was sacked at least four times, twice as a player, twice as a coach, but his insatiable appetite for life and cricket always brought him back. He developed into a lively inswing bowler once he realised that Arthur Wellard would always have the advantage of the wind. His batting was in the Wellard mould but not quite as consistent. In his autobiography he gives us a few glimpses of life as a Somerset cricketer. A professional's wage was meagre, so any ploy to acquire a little more beer money was worth a try. In 1935 at Clacton he decided to pitch camp on the ground right next to the beer tent and proceeded to take nine wickets in the match. Often Bill and Arthur Wellard would share a double bed on away games to save expenses. He recalls one such occasion[3]: 'I had a fright in the early hours of one Sunday morning when I felt something like a pin sticking into me. I turned on the light and gingerly felt halfway down the bed. It was Arthur's set of false teeth. They must have slipped out during the night. We always used to have an extra pint on a Saturday

Bill Andrews, the hand that bowled Bradman – he'd scored 202 at the time.

of this 'tormented genius of cricket', which reveals the inner turmoil of Somerset's greatest home grown batsman. In it he has described the majesty of Gimblett at the crease:

Harold Gimblett was a marvellous cricketer by so many standards. At times his batting, instinctively classical when the mood was right – and more exhilarating than any of his contemporaries – came near to genius. The farmer's son diligently improved his defence, learned how to hook from one of his great idols, Herbert Sutcliffe, and became a stylist who could fashion an innings as handsomely as Palairet once did. His cover drive was even envied by Hammond, though the pair had no natural rapport; the straight six, a mischief maker off the first ball of an innings, was flawless in its ruthless execution[2].

David Foot's book should be compulsory reading for any student of Somerset cricket history.

Maurice Tremlett hitting Tony Lock to leg in 1949. Arthur McIntyre (Derek Taylor's coach at Surrey) is the wicket-keeper. Eric Bedser at first slip. (Central Press Photos).

night.' Times have changed since then. I can report that I have no recollection of Joel Garner and Colin Dredge sharing a bed.

In 1935 a farmer's son from Bicknoller, near Watchet, made the most spectacular debut in cricket history – Harold Gimblett at Frome. Having been rejected by John Daniell after trials at Taunton he hitch-hiked to Frome as a last minute replacement. Going in at number eight with Arthur Wellard's bat he scored a century in 63 minutes. Promoted to open the innings in 1936 he began brilliantly, won two of three Test Caps and went on to make most of the Somerset batting records. However it was the manner in which he scored his runs that made him special. After a long spell in the field Bill Andrews always preferred to relax his weary frame in the confines of the dressing room, but he always went up to the viewing box when Harold was batting – just as today we always make sure we don't miss a Richards innings. David Foot has written a superb biography

After the Second World War Somerset sparkled briefly under E. F. (Bunty) Longrigg. In 1946, with his band of experienced professionals augmented by Johnny Lawrence, a batsman and googly bowler from Yorkshire (later to become a mentor of Geoff Boycott), the side finished fourth with 12 wins. Innings victories over the Indians and Middlesex and three consecutive totals of 500 at Taunton made it a memorable year.

Longrigg was succeeded by R. J. O. Meyer, surely the club's most eccentric captain. An instinctive gambler, both on and off the cricket field, he must also have been blessed with an extremely persuasive tongue. No ordinary mortal could have cajoled a group of experienced professionals to vacate their card schools one rainy day at Taunton and to move their chairs around the pavilion to parade his latest theories about field placings. On another occasion he contrived to rustle up some food for his weary side whilst travelling on the Manchester Express by pulling the communication cord; there is no record of Meyer or the club being fined. He founded Millfield School, one of Somerset's most prolific nurseries.

(Left) Sammy Woods at the beginning of his career . . .

and (below) at the end – 'the most gregarious cricketer of his time.' (Somerset County Gazette).

When Pete Roebuck arrived for his interview he recalls knocking on Meyer's study door:

'As I entered an orange flew towards me. I caught it. "Well done", said Meyer, "but you should have thrown it back." He then took me to a tennis court to bat with a tennis racket to the bowling of my reluctant sister.'[4]

Not only was Pete given a scholarship but his parents were instructed to come to Millfield as full-time teachers. They are still there.

By the early fifties the professionals had begun to run out of steam and Somerset CCC reached its nadir, finishing bottom in four consecutive seasons. The decline caused an outcry from members led by the late Ron Roberts, then a young journalist in Taunton; there were two special general meetings of members and the club reacted by recruiting players from all

(Left) Bill Andrews (1930–47) – a wholehearted, entertaining, thirsty cricketer. (Somerset County Gazette).

(Below) One of Somerset's most successful sides. Back row (from left to right): H. Gimblett, F. S. Lee, A. W. Wellard, R. E. Trump, W. H. R. Andrews, H. T. Buse, J. Lawrence. Front row (from left to right): W. T. Lukes, A. T. M. Jones, N. S. Mitchell-Innes, E. F. Longrigg (capt), C. J. P. Barnwell, G. R. Langdale. (Albert Wilkes).

The Somerset side at the turn of the century – nine amateurs
and two professionals. (Somerset County Gazette).

over the world. Peter Wight, a delightful strokemaker from British Guiana, made a hundred in his first match against the 1953 Australians. Over the next twelve years he mastered all the leading county bowlers with the exception of F. S. Trueman. In 1962 at Taunton, when Trueman was omitted from the Yorkshire side for disciplinary reasons, Peter proceeded to score a brilliant 215. Three experienced Australians were enlisted: in 1956 Colin McCool (aged 41) and J. W. MacMahon (aged 37) arrived and they were joined by Bill Alley (aged 38) in 1957. With some justification Somerset were dubbed 'The League of Nations'.

A second XI was started under the sympathetic guidance of Eric Hill, a former Somerset opener, and the results were most gratifying. Brian Langford and Ken Palmer soon established themselves in the first team along with Graham Atkinson, a Yorkshireman, who joined the club at 13 years of age and became a reliable opener with over 14,000 runs in 12 seasons.

In 1958 Somerset finished third, the club's best performance ever, under the leadership of Maurice Tremlett, who had been appointed the club's first professional captain in 1956. Tremlett's first job was as an office boy at the Taunton headquarters. His first match brought him eight wickets in a thrilling defeat of Middlesex at Lord's in 1947: typically Somerset beat Middlesex again later in the season before they became champions. After two tours with the MCC Tremlett mysteriously lost his ability to bowl and so concentrated upon his attacking batting, also developing into one of the most astute captains in the club's history. As a batsman he must have relished playing on Somerset's short outfields: his speciality was the lofted drive over the bowler's head and often at Taunton the boundary was cleared with what seemed like a golfer's chip shot.

Tremlett was succeeded by Harold Stephenson, Somerset's most successful wicketkeeper, who took over 1,000 dismissals during his sixteen years at the club. He also developed into an effective batsman with a penchant for grabbing daring quick singles which terrified his partners but greatly amused his colleagues back in the pavilion. His infectious enthusiasm for the game ensured that Somerset's improvement since Tremlett's appointment was maintained. From 1962 to 1964 Somerset finished sixth, third and eighth respectively, so that when he handed over the captaincy to Colin Atkinson in 1965 Somerset supporters could expect their side to mount a serious challenge for one of the two trophies now available in county cricket – a rare luxury. However I doubt that any of them anticipated the scenes at Lord's on 2nd September, 1967, when Somerset had their first genuine opportunity to bring a trophy back to Taunton.

Somerset in 1963. Back row (left to right): J. Lawrence, R. C. Kerslake, T. Barwell, L. M. L. Barnwell, F. W. Willetts. Middle row (left to right): A. H. Holman (masseur), P. J. Eele, M. J. Kitchen, R. Robinson, G. Hall, J. D. Martin, C. M. Greetham, B. Roe, T. Tout (scorer). Front row (left to right): K. E. Palmer, G. Atkinson, W. E. Alley, H. W. Stephenson (capt), P. B. Wight, B. A. Langford, R. T. Virgin. (Charrett and Clarke).

1. GILLETTE CUP FINAL, 1967

The 1967 Gillette Cup Final captured the imagination of the Somerset public. The 5,250 tickets allocated to the club were gone within five days. Secretary, Richard Robinson, reckoned that he could have sold three times the miserly Lord's allocation. No doubt there were a few romantic supporters who couldn't come to terms with the possibility of Somerset actually winning a competition, fearing that the lovable reputation of Somerset as gallant, unpredictable losers might be forever tarnished. But as a twelve year-old perched underneath Old Father Time on my first visit to Lord's, a Somerset victory was my only prerequisite for a glorious day out.

Somerset were regarded as the underdogs. After all, their opponents were Kent (runners-up in the Championship in 1967) led by England's sporadic captain, Colin Cowdrey. However, Somerset's appearance in the final was no fluke, but the culmination of a gradual improvement during the sixties. They had finished third in the Championship in 1963 and in 1966, when they registered a record thirteen wins. Also in 1966 they had reached the semi-final of the Gillette Cup, losing to Warwickshire at Edgbaston. So arguably this could be regarded as Somerset's best side to date.

The strength of the side, as in all successful teams, lay in its bowling attack which revolved around Fred Rumsey, Ken Palmer, Brian Langford and Bill Alley. The batting relied heavily upon the Somerset-born duo of Virgin and Kitchen and the evergreen Alley. I wonder how often the selectors rued the premature departures of Graham Atkinson and Peter Wight, one to Lancashire, the other to the umpires' list.

Let's look at a few of the key players in the side:

The county career of Bill Alley must be considered unique in recent times. There is a parallel in Basil D'Oliveira, but he started playing for Worcestershire at the tender age of 30. Bill started his career at Somerset at the age of 38, a time when most county cricketers' wives have glued the final newspaper cutting into the scrapbook. In his youth he had worked on an oyster farm, mixed concrete for the bridge over the Hawkesbury River, north of Sydney, been a boilermaker's assistant, a prizefighter and a bouncer, as well as a state cricketer for New South Wales. He narrowly missed selection for Don Bradman's all-conquering 1948 tour of England – perhaps

because he was too old. Then he tried his luck in the Lancashire League for almost ten years, regularly breaking club records at Colne and Blackpool. So when he arrived at Taunton in 1957 he had every right to feel a little jaded. No one anticipated, except perhaps himself, that he would still be playing in 1968, nor did the Somerset Committee have any reason to expect him to score over 3,000 runs and take 62 wickets in 1961, his benefit year.

In the sixties he became the lynch pin of the side in the manner of Botham in recent England teams. His batting was unorthodox, inelegant but extremely effective. His forward defensive was particularly horrible to watch but he didn't play it very often. He'd long since perfected a wallop over mid-wicket off good length balls which inevitably forced the unfortunate bowler to try bowling bad ones; these might be despatched in more conventional style. Spinners had to be attacked; balls outside the off stump would disappear over square leg, straight deliveries might be late cut past third man. Especially after the departure of Colin McCool and Peter Wight he became Somerset's prime matchwinning batsman, and he never wore a thigh pad!

In contrast to the cavalier nature of his batting, his bowling was niggardly and particularly suited to Gillette Cup cricket. His fourteen-stone frame would glide to the wicket noiselessly and deliver the ball at medium pace; he could swing the ball each way as well as move it off the seam. Only in his later years did a lengthy innings prevent him from bowling sustained accurate spells. As with the likes of Derek Shackleton and Tom Cartwright, no one can ever recall him bowling badly.

In the field the gully became his personal domain and he often took catches that only a superlative natural sportsman could hold. The gully also gave him a permanent audience for the constant chatter that cascaded from his obviously Australian tongue. Bill must be considered the least reticent cricketer ever to have played for Somerset (amidst very strong competition). Canny county captains would issue strict instructions to their fielders never to talk to Alley. Bill would bellow up the wicket to his partner that he'd been sent to Coventry again and, undeterred, would keep talking, cracking jokes and belting the ball to deep mid-wicket. A sense of theatre and fun

The Somerset supporters were determined to enjoy themselves at the 1967 Gillette Cup final.

Colin Atkinson leads Somerset out in the final of 1967. He's flanked by Fred Rumsey, Bill Alley, Mervyn Kitchen (hidden), Graham Burgess and Roy Virgin.

made him a spectator's dream. In his autobiography he recalls one of his many scraps with F. S. Trueman:

I drove Fred's first ball and hooked the next to the boundary, a gesture tantamount to tickling a bush snake. Fred reacted with two bumpers ... the crowd booed and at the end of the over I set them off again by striding down the pitch with the bat raised. Fred played along by striding out to meet me halfway. Suddenly the fans went very quiet as they saw Fred push his face into mine. And out of the corner of his mouth came the promise, 'First pint's on me tonight, Bill.'[5]

Nor could umpires escape his mischievous sense of humour. He recalls a game at Bournemouth when he casually asked the umpire if he was carrying a knife. The umpire obliged and Bill politely asked whether he would open the blade of the knife, which he did.

Bill then took the knife and meticulously started cutting around the new ball, lifting the seam in the process. The umpire, horrorstricken, blurted out a few words about reporting him to Lord's, but was soon silenced when Bill coolly remarked, 'You'd look nice reporting me to Lord's after giving me the knife and standing by my side while I picked the seam.' I'm quite sure that Bill Alley, the Test umpire, would never have fallen for that little ruse.

Fred Rumsey was the spearhead of the bowling attack, the one who could bang the ball around the batsman's earholes if necessary in those far-off helmetless days. Timorous opening batsmen would look for his name first on the scorecard when arriving at the county ground and probably score a hundred if he was absent – perhaps playing for England, as he did five times in 1964/5. He had been an immediate

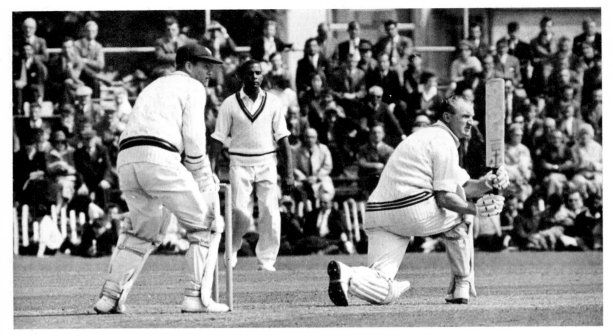

Bill Alley defying the textbook against the touring West Indians in 1963. (Bristol Evening Post/Western Daily Press).

success at Somerset after his departure from Worcestershire, who already boasted an attack of Flavell, Coldwell and Brain.

Off a long, ambling run he bowled left arm over the wicket and fast. He had the priceless ability to swing the ball back into the right-hand batsman but apparently he didn't hit the seam very often. Once Ken Palmer and Bill Alley decided to prove this point on a damp, muddy Taunton practice wicket. Both bowled two overs and produced the evidence of mud in the seam after each successful delivery. Bill hit the seam every time, Ken ten times. The nonplussed Rumsey hit it twice and declared defiantly that he was a fast bowler who didn't have to bother with such intricacies anyway. His record proves him right. In his five seasons with Somerset he captured no less than 445 wickets. He seldom broke down and might have improved England's chances of regaining the Ashes in 1965–6 if he had been preferred to the injury-prone David Larter. He retired from full time cricket at the age of 32 : perhaps he was too intelligent and articulate a man to pound up to the wicket day after day, often on unhelpful surfaces, sweat bursting from every pore. Indeed, he was one of the guiding lights behind the formation of the successful players' union, the Cricketers' Association.

At the other end Ken Palmer, who had joined the staff as a 17 year-old in 1954, proved an admirable foil. Only 5 feet 7 inches tall, his approach to the wicket was rapid, culminating in a whirlwind action that sent the ball skidding down the pitch. If conditions were at all helpful the ball would move either way off the wicket. Such was his ability to make the ball deviate that Colin Atkinson, his captain, preferred not to face him in the nets since he reasoned, quite logically, that all he could achieve was a loss of form and confidence.

Ken was also an accomplished batsman (he achieved the double in 1961), very correct, loath to give his wicket away and particularly adept and courageous against fast bowling – the sort of player who was a reassuring figure going to the wicket at 29 for 5, as he did once at Southport. He proceeded to score 118 in 370 minutes and shepherded the Somerset total to an unexpected 323.

Ken played for England in Port Elizabeth, South Africa, in bizarre circumstances – as a last minute replacement when John Price and Tom Cartwright were injured (he happened to be coaching in Johannesburg at the time). Not that he is a stranger to the Test match scene, having become one of our most respected Test umpires. Nor is he a stranger to

Fred Rumsey, Somerset's spearhead in the sixties. (Bath & Wilts Chronicle & Herald).

Bill Alley opens his shoulders. Elegance was not his prime consideration. (Bill Smith).

Taunton: his enthusiasm and knowledge of the game have benefited a long line of Somerset players in the '70s and '80s. His son, Gary, a carbon copy of Ken 30 years ago, is now on the Somerset staff.

So Colin Atkinson was fortunate to have such a gifted combination of bowlers backed by the accurate off-spin of Brian Langford. The system that evolved in Championship cricket was this: Rumsey would open the bowling with the wind, with Palmer at the other end; Palmer would then use the wind after Rumsey's spell, with Alley bowling into it. Thereafter Brian Langford would operate into the wind with the pace trio rotating at the other end. If the wicket was turning Peter Robinson's slow left arm spinners might be introduced. If the ball was swinging Graham Burgess, Roy Palmer or the captain might bowl a few overs.

In theory it all sounds so simple. I'm sure it wasn't. As Brian Rose will testify, captaining a successful side can be a headache. In a good team there are bound to be strong characters and inevitable personality clashes (think of Yorkshire in the early sixties). So whenever

a side is successful, the captain deserves special credit, particularly when there are doubts about his own playing ability. The Somerset players enterprisingly put together a special brochure in 1967, *Up from Somerset for the Cup*;[6] the fervour aroused by the Cup Final certainly warranted some sort of publication. In it the captain is quoted:

'The main doubt I had about taking the job concerned my own playing ability. I didn't want to be in the side just on sufferance. I just had to be worth my place. I accepted it as a great challenge.'

His record suggests that he overcame this challenge. In 1966 he scored over 1,000 runs, his medium pacers were particularly useful in Gillette Cup games (arthritis had prevented him from continuing as a leg spinner) and he was an excellent fielder.

As captain, he was in the amateur tradition, a schoolmaster at Millfield, given time off by that benevolent headmaster, R. J. O. Meyer. 'C.R.M.' was a great theorist, though never so extreme or unorthodox as his headmaster. Often he would instruct four or five people to be padded up simultaneously to cover any eventuality. 'X' would bat if the left arm spinner was bowling, 'Y' for the off spinner and the unfortunate 'Z' if the hairy quicks were bowling. Peter Robinson, for instance, reckons that he has batted in every position for Somerset.

The captain was prepared to accept the advice of the seasoned professionals on the field with him. Geoff Clayton, the diminutive, independent Lancastrian was, as wicket keeper, in an excellent position to judge the vagaries of the wicket or the batsman. And I'm sure Bill Alley would normally have something to say on the progress of the game. Bill Andrews, the county coach in 1967, emphasises this point in his autobiography:

> During his three years as skipper he recognised me as coach. We used to select the side together, although naturally he had the final word. When we discussed tactics he would listen to me. That made a change from some of the previous Somerset captains.[3]

Colin Atkinson retired at the end of the 1967 season and returned to full-time teaching, but he has continued to serve the club in an administrative capacity, presently fulfilling the role of President with all the dignity one expects of a public school headmaster.

These four crucial members of the team – Colin Atkinson, Bill Alley, Ken Palmer and Fred Rumsey – were soon to disappear from regular county cricket. Other members of the side, such as Roy Virgin, Mervyn Kitchen and the faithful Brian Langford we shall meet later on. It is surprising, considering Brian's later one-day record, that he was never included in the 1967 Gillette side. The vogue was for an all seam

Bill Alley and Ken Palmer – poachers turned gamekeepers.

attack. He accepted this situation philosophically, removed bottle-tops and champagne corks when necessary and continued taking a hatful of wickets in Championship games.

There's no doubt that the system of a barrage of seamers proved very effective in the 1967 Gillette Cup matches. Leicestershire were dismissed for 160 in April, Warwickshire for 181, Northants for 148 – Bill Alley having the remarkable figures 12–6–8–2, ensuring the man of the match award for the second game in succession.

Against Lancashire in the semi-final at Old Trafford, Somerset enjoyed the best of the conditions. Before the toss Colin Atkinson had sent out his senior professional, Langford, and Lancastrian exile, Geoff Clayton, for a preliminary look at the wicket. Somerset won the toss and batted – thankfully. When the Manchester rain inevitably intervened, to the dismay of stoic Somerset supporters, the score was 100 for 2 off 29 overs. Steady batting the following day ensured a reasonable target for Lancashire to chase and the wicket was deteriorating. The seam attack exploited the helpful conditions and Somerset coasted home by 100 runs, Ken Palmer winning the award.

Afterwards Brian Statham, Lancashire's captain, commented: 'When we lost the toss at Old Trafford, we lost the match. But I must give Somerset credit – they took their chances well. They batted better than us, and bowled better. Kent will not find it easy in the Final.'[6]

So all around the county the pursuit for the odd spare ticket began and the players started to prepare themselves for the greatest occasion in Somerset's colourful, but distinctly unsuccessful history.

The stateliest home of English cricket had never experienced the peculiar delights of such a vocally uninhibited crowd as flocked through the Grace Gate early on September 2nd, 1967. It could have been a world heavyweight title contest, as the Somerset supporters in the stands chanted 'All . . . ey, All . . . ey,' before play began. One or two staunch MCC eyebrows must have been raised as odd creatures, clad in white smocks, covered with straw, brandishing barrels of cider, paraded around the boundary. We even had our own pop group, Adge Cutler and the Wurzels, whose masterpiece, 'Drink Up Thee Cider, George', echoed around a bewildered Mound Stand. The Somerset contingent in the crowd were clearly determined to enjoy themselves. Perhaps it wasn't quite so easy for the players.

Colin Cowdrey won the toss and elected to bat on an excellent wicket – not a good omen as Somerset

Somerset in 1967. Standing (left to right): T. Tout (scorer), P. J. Robinson, G. Clayton, A. Clarkson, G. I. Burgess, R. Palmer, L. M. L. Barnwell, T. I. Barwell, M. J. Kitchen, F. T. Willetts, A. H. Holman (masseur). Seated (left to right): R. T. Virgin, W. E. Alley, W. H. R. Andrews (coach), C. R. M. Atkinson (capt), B. A. Langford, K. E. Palmer, F. E. Rumsey. (L. G. Charrett).

had won all their previous matches fielding second. A photo of Colin Atkinson leading the side out reveals the tension on the players' faces: even Bill Alley is silent and grim-faced. For the bulk of the side, performing in front of 25,000 spectators was definitely a new experience.

The pre-lunch session was a disaster. The Palmer brothers were uncharacteristically wayward amd Mike Denness was particularly severe on any loose deliveries. At lunch Kent had reached 129 for 1 off 34 overs, and even the naïve optimism of a twelve year-old was sorely tested.

After lunch there was a complete transformation. I wish this could be attributed to a Churchillian oration from the captain and to the entire side downing a couple of pints of scrumpy with their salads, but, however hard I try, I can't find any players involved able to support this theory. Whatever happened, Kent began to collapse dramatically against the persistence of Alley, Rumsey and a realigned Ken Palmer. I remember well the standing ovation given to Colin Cowdrey, recently appointed as England's captain to tour the West Indies, and the second of stunned silence soon afterwards as he was brilliantly caught by Peter Robinson at mid-wicket.

Some of the Somerset supporters must have found the afternoon session rather demanding. One group had decided to sink a pint of cider at the fall of each Kent wicket. After a morning of almost complete abstinence, they were suddenly required to sup nine pints in the space of ninety minutes. Being of stout

Somerset stock they refused to be overwhelmed by their task.

Suddenly everything had clicked into place, the bowlers had become miserly and the fielding brilliant. Six wickets fell for 21 runs in 13 overs and, to everyone's surprise, Kent were dismissed for 193. At tea we were 51 for 0 and I had difficulty digesting my ham sandwiches. Peter Robinson, in particular, was playing with remarkable freedom, especially when you consider that he'd spent most of the season batting at number nine. A successful experiment during the Weston Festival (never the easiest place to score runs) had ensured him the opening position and this was confirmed by a career-best 97 against Middlesex in the game before the final. On his own admission he was a 'bit of a blocker', but no one would have guessed it.

But this was to prove a game of sessions, and the final one belonged emphatically to Kent. After tea Somerset were becalmed. Peter Robinson recalls, 'Roy got impatient: Mervyn went well to keep us in the hunt until a brilliant return catch dismissed him unluckily and I had a flash.' Bill Alley received an ovation akin to Cowdrey's: he would dearly have loved to be Somerset's saviour on this day, but he was soon snapped up by Alan Brown on the legside. A youthful Graham Burgess and the talented Terry Barwell then momentarily revived Somerset's spirits, 27 runs coming from four overs. But then, as the disconsolate reporter of the *Somerset County Gazette* recorded, 'Barwell was tragically run out completing

Ken Palmer on the attack. (Somerset County Gazette).

You can see the seam; a good sign as Ken Palmer bowls against Kent. (Somerset County Gazette).

Somerset v Kent, Gillette Cup Final
2nd September, 1967

KENT

M. H. Denness, c Clayton b Alley	50
B. W. Luckhurst, c Atkinson b Alley	54
J. Shepherd, c Virgin b Rumsey	30
*M. C. Cowdrey, c Robinson b K. E. Palmer	1
†A. P. E. Knott, run out	21
A. L. Dixon, b Alley	0
S. E. Leary, c Clayton b R. Palmer	1
A. Brown, c Barwell b R. Palmer	1
A. Ealham, run out	17
D. L. Underwood, b R. Palmer	7
J. N. Graham, not out	0
Extras (b1, l-b 8, n-b 2)	11
	193

Fall of wickets: 1/78, 2/138, 3/141, 4/145, 5/147, 6/148, 7/150, 8/177, 9/187.
Bowling: Rumsey 12–1–28–1; K. E. Palmer 12–3–37–1; R. Palmer 10.4–0–53–3; Alley 12–4–22–3; Atkinson 7–1–25–0; Burgess 6–2–17–0.

SOMERSET

R. Virgin, c Graham b Dixon	17
P. J. Robinson, c Knott b Shepherd	48
M. J. Kitchen, c and b Dixon	15
T. I. Barwell, run out	24
W. E. Alley, c Brown b Shepherd	8
G. Burgess, c Knott b Brown	27
*C. R. M. Atkinson, c Luckhurst b Underwood	1
†G. Clayton, b Underwood	8
K. E. Palmer, c Luckhurst b Underwood	0
R. Palmer, c Leary b Graham	2
F. E. Rumsey, not out	1
Extras (l-b 8, n-b 2)	10
	161

Fall of wickets: 1/58, 2/84, 3/84, 4/102, 5/129, 6/131, 7/144, 8/145, 9/152.
Bowling: Graham 12–4–26–1; Brown 9.5–3–20–1; Underwood 10–2–41–3; Shepherd 12–2–27–2; Dixon 11–2–37–2.

Kent won by 32 runs

---

almost two runs while his partner sat steadfastly on his bat at the bowler's end.' Even I realised that the situation was now hopeless. Graham Burgess swung desperately but ran out of partners, and Kent were home by 32 runs in what *Wisden* described as 'probably the best of all the five final ties.'[7] The 92-year wait for a trophy had to continue.

Peter Robinson, top scorer at Lord's; now the club's coach.

Roy Palmer, who has now joined his brother on the umpire's line (S & G Press Agency).

2. 1968–70

During the following three years there were very few indications for Somerset's followers that the long wait would ever come to an end. In 1968, Roy Kerslake, who had played for Cambridge University in 1963–4, was appointed captain. It was to be a difficult summer for him. Initially he was hampered by injury, and in addition his innate modesty and selflessness prevented him from allowing his considerable talents to blossom. A capable all-rounder, he bowled only 39 overs in the season and batted at number seven. Moreover the backbone of the side during the previous five years, its bowling attack, was beginning to feel the strain. Ken Palmer was beset by injuries and Bill Alley was in his fiftieth year. Somerset finished twelfth in the Championship. Roy left the game to continue his work as a solicitor but was to make far greater contributions to Somerset cricket beyond the boundary ropes in the years to come.

He was succeeded by Brian Langford, the senior professional. He had joined the staff way back in 1952 as a batsman/seam bowler and within fifteen months had found himself top of the national bowling averages as an off-spinner. He made his debut in Bertie Buse's infamous benefit match against Lancashire at Bath which was completed in a day. In the next game, against Kent, he took fourteen wickets followed by eleven against Leicestershire. In his first three games he had taken 26 wickets for 308 runs. Just in case you start diving into the record books to look up my record at this haven of spinners, I'd like to point out that the wickets at Bath have changed a little – at least, in my opinion. Nonetheless, not a bad start for a seventeen year-old making his way in the game.

After his national service Brian returned to the full-time staff in 1956 and became an ever present member of the side for almost twenty years. He played for the MCC three years in succession from 1958 but international honours just eluded him. Perhaps he was unlucky to play for an unfashionable county, but also the competition for off-spinning places was extremely fierce with Titmus, Allen, Mortimer and Illingworth all available. Maybe if his generous easy-going nature had included a hard streak of ruthlessness he would have won a cap, but I wonder whether he would have thought it worthwhile.

His greatest asset was his control. In 1974 I remember Brian Close sending for 'Langie' when Tom Cartwright had been injured. Immediately, after no practice, he was able to drop onto an impeccable length and to bowl long, accurate spells. He was not a big spinner of the ball but, to use the professional's phraseology, he 'did enough'. His colleagues cannot remember many occasions when he didn't 'do his job' on the rain-affected wickets of the sixties. He was also known as a fine spinner on good wickets, the real test of a bowler's craft. This was because he bowled so accurately that he could dictate to the batsman into which area of the field he would have to hit the ball: naturally this area would be well policed by the best fielders and the batsman, frustrated, would be forced into error.

Brian Langford holds one record that can never be bettered. In 1969 at Yeovil, in the John Player League, I saw him bowl eight overs, eight maidens. Keith Boyce, of Essex, faced one ball of this spell. He attempted to hit it out of Johnson Park, failed and a leg-bye was given. I've heard it whispered that the ball may have just brushed his glove, but I dismiss it

Roy Kerslake, captain in 1968.

29

A fresh-faced Greg Chappell delighted the Somerset crowds for two years. (Somerset County Gazette).

as an ugly rumour. To use another common cricketer's phrase, 'look in the book'.

'Langie' was also a capable lower order batsman. Given a choice, he preferred the bowling to be of medium pace or below, but of course we all do. The only difference was that Brian was prepared to admit this quite openly, sometimes to the square leg umpire. Fortunately, since he retired he has been a regular visitor to the county ground and has been a sympathetic and invaluable guide to me, especially when the groundstaff have been frantically trying to recover balls that have come to rest in St James' Churchyard or the sleepy river Tone.

So to Brian Langford fell the onerous task of captaining Somerset in 1969 with a skeleton staff of thirteen, when just one Championship victory was gained. The side was ill balanced, lacking a penetrating opening attack; the batsmen invariably found themselves batting to save the game rather than win it, always a demoralizing task. A youthful Greg Chappell had been signed in 1968 and he gave many glimpses of the imperious batsman who was to emerge in the Australian sides of the seventies. Two shy, blond locals, Peter Denning and Brian Rose, were blooded in the most trying of circumstances. But the main burden fell upon the two established home-grown players of contrasting styles, Roy Virgin and Mervyn Kitchen.

Roy Virgin was a great accumulator who solidly scored his thousand runs every year, relying on his ability to drive on the off side and tuck the ball away to leg. He played for Somerset for almost ten years in this vein. Suddenly in 1970 he went berserk. He belted the ball everywhere, scored twice his normal quota of runs and narrowly missed England selection. Strangely, he never managed to repeat his 1970 form. I'm sure that Roy, like all cricketers, tried to analyse what causes sudden success or failure, but the answer remains maddeningly elusive. Anyway Roy returned to being an extremely competent opening batsman rather than a dominant matchwinner. In 1972 he became one of the few players to leave the club before the end of their career, when he moved to Northamptonshire. For a decade Somerset had been indebted to his consistency and his insatiable appetite for runs.

Of course, like all batsmen, he suffered the agonies of a long run of failures. In 1972 he travelled to Worcester far from confident, his mind ill at ease. When it came to his turn to bat, he could be seen

Brian Langford, captain in 1969–71, bowls to Arthur Milton. (Bristol Evening Post/Western Daily Press).

A typical Kitchen square cut. (S & G Press Agency).

striding on to the playing area immaculate as ever, pads and boots carefully whitened, his Somerset cap fixed, but no bat. When someone generously mentioned this little oversight, Roy dashed back to the pavilion, retrieved his willow and returned to the wicket. He took guard and decided to leave his first ball. Unfortunately it was straight, Virgin was bowled and sorrowfully set off on that long, humiliating journey back to the pavilion wondering, amongst other things, whether his cigarette had gone out.

His friend and rival Mervyn Kitchen played in a different vein. If the mood was right and his touch sure he could be a devastating player with all the shots, but particularly strong square on the off side. Most long Kitchen innings were memorable. Perhaps his finest was in a losing cause against Lancashire in the Gillette Cup in 1972. He pillaged 116 out of 194 as Somerset failed to reach their goal by nine runs.

He was an extremely good chaser of targets. This made him a favourite player to bat with as he could judge the tempo of an innings perfectly and was always eager to snatch singles for the new batsmen by alert running. It was reassuring to know that Mervyn would scamper up to your end even if there was a six-foot West Indian with toothache bowling at the time.

Off the field he was remarkably pessimistic. With one run to win, two hours to spare, six wickets in hand and a cloudless sky, Merv would grudgingly admit to a chance of victory. On a dicey wicket his false teeth would be unceremoniously removed for safe keeping. In fact I think his teeth escaped unscathed throughout his career, but Mike Procter did have a rather annoying habit of hitting him on the nose. Leaving the dressing room at Bristol, Mervyn would snatch one last fleeting glimpse of his nose, wonder about its wellbeing for a second and then set off to bat with the intense commitment he shows in whatever he does, playing cricket for Somerset, football for Taunton Town, or, as now, umpiring in first class cricket.

John Arlott, as usual, summed him up best when he wrote that, 'Some cricketers seem to personify their counties and to see Mervyn Kitchen in the field or at the crease is to recognise him as a Somerset man. His rosy red face, drolly humorous expression, ample seat, rolling walk and rich accent are unmistakably those of a West Countryman.'[8]

It was obvious that reinforcements were needed for our West Countrymen. Derek Taylor from Surrey, Allan Jones from Sussex and Tom Cartwright from Warwickshire were enlisted and their presence ensured a steady improvement in 1970 (Somerset reaching the semi-finals of the Gillette Cup). The process continued in 1971 when from contrasting parts of the globe there emerged Hallam Moseley (Barbados), Kerry O'Keeffe (Sydney) and one D. B. Close from Rawdon, Yorkshire.

Brian Langford – 1,400 wickets for Somerset.

Roy Virgin, dependable opening batsman. Greg Chappell, his teammate in 1968 and 1969, is at first slip.

3. 1971-73

It was all Bill Andrews' idea. As soon as he'd heard of Brian Close's controversial sacking by Yorkshire he started writing letters and making repeated telephone calls inviting Close to Somerset. Once Bill has decided on a course of action he's impossible to divert. Close then visited Somerset and became aware of the poor financial state of the club, but also of the general enthusiasm and eagerness to progress. Within a few days he rang Somerset and accepted their offer.

In his autobiography, *I Don't Bruise Easily*,[9] he describes his desolation on being sacked at Yorkshire. 'The bottom had suddenly dropped out of my world. My consciousness told me that the greatest, most overwhelming disaster of my life was taking place, yet my mind couldn't grasp the enormity of it all.' Somerset provided a new lease of life, a massive contrast to Yorkshire and an opportunity to prove his critics wrong.

In 1971 he played under Brian Langford and thoroughly enjoyed himself. He topped the batting averages and scored five centuries, one against Yorkshire – to no one's surprise. At Yorkshire, with its formidable batting strength, he had grown accustomed to shuffling up and down the order to fill in for absent Test players; at Somerset he was now required to be the main runscorer. He relished this new type of responsibility. It is worth noting that during his time at Somerset he averaged 38 compared with 30 at Yorkshire.

I feel privileged to have batted with him. He didn't say much. Occasionally he might bolster your confidence with this observation of the opposition's best bowler: 'I can play him all right but you might struggle, lad.' Most striking was his intense concentration and determination. Like Vivian Richards at his hungriest, every ounce of energy was directed towards dominating the bowler even if he was in a defensive mood. The possibility of being dismissed wasn't even considered. Peter Roebuck, in *Slices of Cricket*, observed that when the impossible did happen he 'could produce endless explanations for dismissal ranging from forgetting his chewing gum or wearing the wrong boots to stupid partners or foolish spectators jumping up and down as the bowler bowled.'[4] And, of course, he was incredibly brave, whether charging Wes Hall at Lord's in 1963 or receiving a buffeting

from Michael Holding at Old Trafford in 1976. I can remember when 'Closey' returned from Old Trafford to play in a Gillette game against Warwickshire. Early in his innings he was hit by a vicious bouncer from Bob Willis. He buckled and fell. 'Enough is enough,' we all thought. Close went on to top score in the Somerset innings. His example and bravery were to leave a lasting impression on us all.

He was asked to lead the side in 1972. Inevitably he was unable to steer clear of some sort of controversy, even at Somerset. At Swansea in June Somerset played Glamorgan in, to quote *Wisden*, 'a controversial and unpleasant match, in which W. Wooller, the Glamorgan Secretary and D. B. Close, the Somerset captain, were the central figures.'[10] On a shortened first day's play Somerset crawled to 113 for 2 in 72 overs. Close, who scored a century, delayed his declaration until three o'clock the following day, a decision which so incensed the redoubtable Wilf Wooller that he announced to the small crowd that any spectator could have his money back on application. Newspapermen and TV cameras started to descend upon Swansea. Somerset then proceeded to bowl Glamorgan out twice, thanks to the wiles of Cartwright, Langford and O'Keeffe, winning the game by an innings and 25 runs. There was no happier man than Brian Close driving across the Severn Bridge that evening.

Whilst Close was bolstering the batting, Tom Cartwright carried the bowling: two seasoned professionals with very contrasting approaches to the game. Where Close, as a player and captain, might be instinctive and unorthodox, Cartwright was thorough and methodical; he relied upon long periods of pressure to gain his wickets rather than Close's inspired gambits. Once Close decided to bowl Richard Cooper, a rotund hitter from Wiltshire, in a Benson and Hedges match at Gloucestershire. Richard, a confident man, assured the captain that he bowled off spinners fairly regularly for Malmesbury. Off a two pace run up he bowled a couple of no balls, followed by a massive full toss which Mike Procter contrived to mishit to cover. The catch unfortunately was dropped: a Close coup had just failed. Even if it had succeeded, I think Tom would have remained a little uneasy about the Captain's choice of bowler.

Richard Cooper, attacking batsman and occasional off spinner.

One thing they had in common was the greatest respect for each other's ability. Close regarded Tom as 'a joy to watch as a bowler, a supreme artist, a master of accuracy of variation and total concentration and he did a great deal to teach our bowlers a new set of values.'[9] I can remember fielding at forward short leg for Tom and feeling as safe as a glass of water in the members' bar.

Tom was the perfect bowling machine with a classical action. On a wicket that was beginning to crumble he could dig his own holes on a good length

Hallam Moseley at the nets soon after his arrival at Somerset in 1971.

Bill Andrews' dream comes true. Brian Close signs for Somerset, secretary Jimmy James looks on. (Somerset County Gazette).

Brian Close never expected to be dismissed – unless he forgot his chewing gum.

his former employers, Sussex, discovered at Hove in 1973 when he took a career best 9 for 51.

Kerry O'Keeffe, the young Australian mystery man, spent two chequered years at Somerset (1971–2). Initially his mixture of leg spinners, top spinners and googlies bamboozled county batsmen on the early season wickets at Taunton. Cartwright and O'Keeffe would provide a contrasting and exacting challenge for wicket keeper Derek Taylor as well as opponents. For a while Derek coped far more convincingly. Sadly in 1972 Kerry lost all the confidence which is so essential for wrist spinners, had a disastrous year and did not fulfil his three-year contract.

Tom Cartwright – the perfect bowling machine. (Somerset County Gazette).

as each ball would monotonously pitch on the offending spot. He was so accurate that at medium pace he bowled without a third man or long leg: he was too straight to allow batsmen the liberty of scoring behind the wicket. Brian Close would be prowling at forward short leg, Derek Taylor up at the wicket awaiting the snick or the leg side stumping. In four seasons Tom took nearly 400 wickets, topping the national bowling averages in 1973.

Supporting him was Allan Jones, the side's temperamental fast bowler. Allan could be relied upon to finish bottom of the batting averages each year. He looked a little out of place on a cricket field – unless he was bowling. Neither his batting nor his fielding suggested a natural sportsman. His gangling frame and sparrow's legs didn't help the image. Despite all this he possessed a smooth, rhythmic action with a high arm only marred by a loud grunt as he searched for extra pace. On his day he could be very hostile, as

However, the other overseas player, Hallam Moseley, came to stay. His athletic fielding and exotic batting, as well as his fast bowling, made an immediate impression at Taunton. From a whirlwind of arms and legs quick away swingers would emerge, which were hard enough to hit even if you could detect where the ball was coming from. Of course there were teething problems for a Barbadian suddenly pitched into rural England. Communicating with his team was one. On arriving at Taunton one colleague asked Hallam whether he batted left or right handed, only to receive the bewildering answer, 'Half past ten.' In a benefit game he strolled innocently into a large clump of stinging nettles to retrieve the ball, with disastrous but hilarious results. Since then Hallam has become a firm favourite of the Somerset crowd and more conversant with the pitfalls of West Country life.

From Northamptonshire in 1973 came Dennis Breakwell, left arm spinner, dashing batsman and speedy outfielder. Known frequently in the dressing room as 'Twitch', Dennis didn't bother to try to hide his nerves: to calm them he cracked a continuous stream of absolutely horrendous jokes, which somehow seemed to keep everyone amused rather than demented. In stark contrast was 'Gentleman' Jim Parks who played his last two years of cricket at Somerset, always unruffled and still oozing class.

So with a steady stream of experienced imports, Somerset became a more competitive side, capable of upsetting the best. From 1971 to 1973 they occupied respectable mid-table positions in the Championship and the John Player League. But there wasn't an endless supply of experienced county cricketers on the market. Recruiting them could only be a short term measure. Anyway, Roy Kerslake, now Chairman of the Cricket Committee, had some other ideas.

The ever-popular Hallam Moseley

Jim Parks finished his career at Somerset.

4. 1974

In the winter of 1973 Roy Kerslake distributed a paper to the members of the General Committee advocating that Somerset should adopt a youth policy. This would obviously entail extra expense for the club, not necessarily in terms of mammoth salary increases (my first wage was £15 a week) but in enlarging the second XI fixture list to include the team in both the Minor Counties and the second XI competitions. His proposals were readily accepted.

So, in April 1974, those reporting for duty included for the first time Ian Botham, Peter Roebuck, Phil Slocombe, John Hook, Vic Marks and a West Indian whose big hitting for Lansdown had raised a few eyebrows. I remember watching Viv Richards smash the first ball he received in a middle practice to the square cover boundary. Peter Roebuck and I nodded sagely at one another and came to the conclusion that we might struggle to squeeze into the first team ahead of this gentleman from Antigua.

Most of us had arrived at the county ground by conventional routes. Ian had spent two years terrorizing the Lord's groundstaff. The others had played under the watchful eyes of Reg Pitman and Bill Andrews in Somerset youth sides. Viv Richards' path to Somerset was less orthodox.

Early in 1973 Len Creed, successful Bath bookmaker and Somerset Vice-Chairman, was visiting Antigua with Norman Teer's Mendip Acorns. In his wallet he carried a cutting from *The Cricketer* in which Colin Cowdrey had noted that 'there was a chap called Vivian Richards who looked promising.' Len met Viv and watched him scoring a quick 30 with the assistance of the home umpire, who realized the importance of this particular game for Viv. Len was impressed and phoned Colin Atkinson, Somerset's Chairman.

Colin was understandably cautious. He recalls:

When Len rang first seeking the necessary authority to bring his discovery back I didn't want to involve the county club in unnecessary expense and I was reluctant to use up a special registration on the recommendation of one man. He rang a second time. Would we, he now wondered, be agreeable for him to bring Vivian over on the understanding that if the newcomer was good enough, we'd

reimburse him? It seemed a very good and fair deal. I said 'Yes'.[11]

As David Foot remarks in the introduction to Viv's autobiography, it was 'a remarkable piece of opportunism, judgement and financial courage.'[11] Viv's record with Lansdown in 1973 soon convinced Somerset that Len Creed's hunch was a winner. Never bet against a bookmaker.

I remember arriving, wide-eyed and scrupulously punctual, for my first day's work for Somerset CCC and being struck by the inactivity. Inevitably it was pouring with rain. So the morning was spent discussing non-cricketing matters. Were the expenses for food and petrol acceptable? Probably not. Would they give more? Probably not. It hadn't occurred to me that cricketers would be concerned about how much they earned. Bargaining and industrial disputes, in my little world, were confined to massive factories in Dagenham.

When the rain eased, tracksuits were donned, a few laps completed and then down to the serious business: football—it was too wet for nets anyway. The fiercely competitive nature of the games startled me; arguments raged, decisions were disputed. I shouldn't have been so surprised. A bunch of professional sportsmen are extremely reluctant to concede anything at tiddlywinks. Even now I discover that I lose at snap to my three-year-old daughter with grave misgivings.

In 1974 the age of the tracksuit cricketer had just about arrived. At Wellington Sports Centre weights were tossed around and devious training circuits were completed. Innocent dog walkers would be confronted by a motley line of tracksuits of differing shapes and sizes heading resolutely for Wellington's monument. Nowadays it is reassuring to know that Dennis Waight, our physio/trainer, knows exactly what he's doing with us. Whatever he demands will be of definite value. We were never quite so sure in 1974. In the afternoon were recreational activities. These might range from carpet bowls to water polo. As goalkeeper at the deep end I produced my most courageous sporting achievement to date, despite our side losing 13–2. I'm a complete non-swimmer.

To be in the same dressing room as Brian Close,

Viv has developed into a dangerous medium pacer.

ex-England captain and 25 years a professional, was a great thrill. On my first trip Closey asked me if I could sandpaper his bat whilst the side was fielding. I found a bat bearing the initials 'D.B.' and set about cleaning it with gusto. I was eager to please my new captain and the bat was lovingly tended. My pride soon disintegrated when the side returned to the pavilion. A puzzled Dennis Breakwell picked up his spotless Stuart Surridge and then thanked me for my unsolicited efforts.

Once the 'real' cricket started Viv Richards dismissed any doubts that Len Creed or Brian Close may have harboured. At Swansea on April 27, in his

Len Creed, the Bath bookmaker who brought Viv Richards to Somerset.

very first game, he scored 81 not out, shepherding Somerset to victory with fourteen overs to spare. Charlie Barnett presented him with the Benson & Hedges Gold award. The whole side descended to the bottom of the pavilion steps to applaud his debut in English county cricket. One innings was sufficient for the Somerset players to realise that Len Creed had unearthed a genius. Brian Close delivered the immortal words, 'You'll do for me, lad.' It was all too much for Len Creed, who was crying.

Ian Botham quickly became a regular member of the team. The new recruits always made sure that they were watching when he was batting. We knew he could smash the ball hard. We wanted to see him do it in the first team; anything might happen. His first Championship innings tended to be exciting but

brief. Occasionally he was employed as a nightwatchman. Almost ten years later we still make the trip to the balcony when Ian is batting and we're still never sure what's going to happen. Of course his innings usually last a little longer now.

It was also in the Benson & Hedges Competition that Ian revealed to the public at large that Somerset had recruited a special cricketer, in the June 12, 1974, quarter final against Hampshire at Taunton. Hampshire, who had already trounced Somerset in the preliminary rounds of the competition, won the toss and batted. Richards and Greenidge sedately scored 22, whereupon four wickets fell. Botham bowled a disbelieving Barry Richards who stayed at the crease, thinking that Derek Taylor had inadvertently removed the bails. It's interesting to recall that at this stage of his career Ian bowled at no more than military medium pace. Trevor Jesty and Peter Sainsbury staged a recovery and Hampshire reached a respectable 182. This target appeared out of reach as Somerset slumped to 113 for 8 with Botham and Moseley at the wicket.

As Eric Hill has recalled, the Press were already completing their reports – Hampshire cruising to

Viv and Ian, two cricketing giants in one dressing room. (Somerset County Gazette).

At Bath it's difficult to relax in the dressing room, but Viv finds a way. (Somerset County gazette).

victory, Trevor Jesty man of the match. Andy Roberts, the quickest bowler in county cricket, was recalled to stifle any last-ditch resistance. The score reached 150, Roberts bounced Botham; the ball hit him in the face and loosened some teeth, but he would continue. Another bouncer was avoided. The Somerset faithful disapproved, booing and jeering Viv's unsmiling Antiguan friend. Hampshire were obviously becoming a little concerned. Botham just cleared Roberts at long leg as he clipped Mike Taylor, Derek's twin, for six. The crowd suddenly sensed the possibility of victory. Complete silence greeted every ball. I was operating the scorebox with Pete Roebuck and vividly remember being corrected by 7,000 spectators as we miscalculated the number of overs bowled. The scorer's telephone was ringing incessantly as in the excitement we lost control of our task (neither of us were to read mathematics at university, anyway).

With 52 overs gone, 168 runs scored, Botham hits Herman for six over the Priory Bridge entrance. With just seven to win Moseley's marvellous innings is ended by a Roberts yorker. Enter Bob Clapp, six foot five, fast bowler, gentle humorist, mediocre batsman. A thunderous appeal for a run out is survived. Eric Hill takes up the story[12]:

> Herman to Botham with two overs to go and three wanted. Botham pushed the first for a long single which he turned down. He went to drive the next and missed. The next was played quietly. The next two he went to drive and missed. Off the last ball Herman came rushing in, Botham flowed beautifully into his cover drive. The pair scampered like creatures possessed; the ball went to the boundary.

The scoreboard never registered Somerset's victory. Charlie Barnett again presented the Man of the Match award, this time to Ian. Could he ever reproduce that sort of performance, we wondered?

In more tranquil circumstances Peter Roebuck also made his debut as an opener at the Weston Festival and impressed everyone whilst making a confident 46 against Warwickshire. He didn't open again for Somerset until 1982 but was soon to establish himself at Cambridge and in the Somerset middle order.

1974 proved to be an exciting season for Somerset supporters as the club came close to glory in the three

Ian Botham – thinking? (Somerset County Gazette).

Ian Botham – striving for pace. (Somerset County Gazette).

Ian Botham in a familiar pose, smashing a boundary ...
(Somerset County Gazette).

Botham receives his county cap from Close. Despite occasional dramatic rows, they developed a deep respect for one another. (Somerset County Gazette).

(Below) Ian Botham – sharing a joke with Trevor Gard and Viv Richards. (Somerset County Gazette).

Another six for Viv? (Somerset County Gazette).

one-day competitions. Semi-finals were lost in the Benson & Hedges and Gillette competitions to Leicester and Kent respectively. Victory in the last John Player League game might have ensured the title but rain intervened at Leicester. All this had

---

Somerset v Hampshire, Benson & Hedges Quarter Final, 12th May, 1974

HAMPSHIRE

B. A. Richards, b Botham	13
C. G. Greenidge, c Cartwright b Burgess	9
D. R. Turner, run out	0
*R. M. C. Gilliat, c Moseley b Burgess	0
T. E. Jesty, c Burgess b Moseley	79
P. J. Sainsbury, c Richards b Botham	40
R. V. Lewis, c Taylor b Clapp	25
M. N. S. Taylor, c Taylor b Moseley	0
†G. R. Stephenson, run out	0
A. M. F. Roberts, c Taylor b Moseley	4
R. S. Herman, not out	6
Extras (l-b 1, w 5)	6

53.3 overs   182

Fall of wickets: 1/22, 2/22, 3/22, 4/22, 5/117, 6/157, 7/158, 8/171, 9/173.

Bowling: Clapp 10–0–43–1; Moseley 10.3–2–28–3; Botham 11–3–33–2; Burgess 11–1–52–2; Cartwright 11–4–20–0.

SOMERSET

M. J. Kitchen, c Gilliat b Herman	5
†D. J. S. Taylor, c Richards b Taylor	33
P. W. Denning, b Jesty	11
I. V. A. Richards, c Stephenson b Jesty	1
*D. B. Close, b Roberts	28
J. M. Parks, c Herman b Jesty	9
G. I. Burgess, lbw b Sainsbury	13
T. W. Cartwright, c Herman b Jesty	0
I. T. Botham, not out	45
H. R. Moseley, lbw b Roberts	24
R. J. Clapp, not out	0
Extras (b 1, l-b 12, n-b 2)	15

9 wickets   54 overs   184

Fall of wickets: 1/9, 2/33, 3/37, 4/85, 5/89, 6/113, 7/113, 8/113, 9/176.

Bowling: Roberts 10–2–26–2; Herman 11–1–40–1; Taylor 11–1–50–1; Jesty 11–2–28–4; Sainsbury 11–2–25–1.

Somerset won by one wicket

Somerset's soccer is taken very seriously. (Somerset County Gazette).

been achieved with Tom Cartwright often out of the side through injury. The emergence of Richards and Botham and the one-day performances of Peter Denning had compensated for this loss and Somerset found an unlikely hero in the one-day competitions in the shape of Bob Clapp, a schoolmaster from Weston.

Cynics suggested that he was successful because the batsman – as well as Bob himself – had no idea where the ball would land. He was better than that. With an ungainly run up which didn't improve aesthetically when he delivered the ball, he took a record 34 wickets in the John Player League, a reward for his persistence and enthusiasm. In the first team he was a nervous cricketer. I can imagine the mental torture he must have experienced waiting to follow the Botham/Moseley partnership in the Benson & Hedges quarter final against Hampshire. He was a joy to play with in the second team. With the pressures removed he would enliven proceedings on a dull day at Salisbury by going out to bat with a set of false Dracula-style teeth in his mouth. Tight-lipped he'd take guard as his arch-rival and friend John Savin pounded in for Wiltshire. Just before the point of delivery he would reveal a distorted toothy grin and

wait for the assembled throng to recover themselves.

Not that we played too many drab second XI matches. Roy Kerslake, who usually captained the side, always kept the game open whenever possible. He was prone to misjudge the time of stumps and miscalculate his declaration accordingly. The opposition might have an hour's more batting than he'd anticipated. Two-day cricket can be very tedious, but Roy always seemed to engineer something and all of us are grateful that we were encouraged to play purposeful cricket.

If we were in danger of becoming bored Steve Wilkinson might come to our rescue. Steve had been a prolific batsman on the Lord's groundstaff and was on Somerset's staff for three years. Steve had one major problem as a professional cricketer: he didn't really like playing cricket. Nothing brought him greater pleasure than the sight of storm clouds gathering over the Quantocks. His main ambition was to become a bookmaker. If play was tedious Steve would offer bets on anything – the number of runs off a particular over, the chances of a wicket being taken or of an earthquake swallowing up first slip. It helped pass the time and Steve never lost. He now runs a successful betting business.

Brian Rose after a brilliant Gillette Cup century against
Derbyshire in 1977. (Somerset County Gazette).

5. 1975–77

The final three years of Close's regime were full of incident but still no trophies. In 1975 results were disappointing but there were compensations, notably the emergence of Phil Slocombe. From the trusted route of Weston Grammar School, Millfield and Somerset youth teams, he established himself in the side, scoring 1,000 runs in his first full season. His neat, uncomplicated batting and brilliant outfielding impressed everyone, including the selectors who picked him for the MCC at the start of 1976. Peter Roebuck returned from the Varsity match, having scored 150 against the luckless Oxford University attack, to compile runs consistently. Brian Rose had established himself as a solid opening batsman. V. J. Marks made his debut for Somerset and made 0 against Hampshire.

In 1976 our main interest lay in the John Player League. If Somerset could beat Glamorgan in the final match of the season, the title was won. To have reached this stage was praiseworthy enough; Richards had been absent all season slaying English bowlers for the West Indies; Brian Close had missed several games because of his remarkable recall to the England team. Moreover three of the first four Sunday league games had been lost, but a series of brilliant batting performances had given Somerset the chance of its first title. Perhaps the most remarkable victory had been at Trent Bridge. Chasing 209, Somerset slumped to 116 for 7, whereupon Keith Jennings and Dennis Breakwell produced a brilliant unbeaten stand of 95, bringing victory with three balls to spare. There would have been plenty of broad smiles in the Globe at Milverton that night.

Much of the side's success had stemmed from the consistency of the opening pair, Rose and Denning.

Somerset and Gloucestershire players bid farewell to Brian Close, 1977. (Somerset County Gazette).

Phil Slocombe made an immediate impact in 1975. (Somerset County Gazette).

Brian Rose and Peter Denning began their Somerset careers together during the slump of the late sixties. It was a tough baptism: often they found themselves batting in hopeless situations or carrying out the arduous, soul destroying task of twelfth man for weeks on end. This experience was to instil in both of them a deep determination to play in a successful Somerset side. Having survived those dark days success has been all the sweeter for them.

They proved to be an ideal opening pair, especially in one-day games. Both were exceedingly quick between the wickets: they stole singles without a sound; a look was sufficient. Their techniques also complemented one another, Rose favouring the leg side, Denning the off. Identical balls would be clipped wide of mid on by Rose and cut to square cover by Denning – all rather bewildering for any inexperienced opening bowler.

'Dasher' Denning is more obviously a butcher's son from Chewton Mendip than a product of Millfield School. He is unmistakably a Somerset man. East of Bristol people struggle to understand him – not that he talks much to 'foreigners' anyway. His favourite musicians are the Wurzels, with or without Adge. He prefers to listen to them at full volume, either on the balcony at Canterbury or while passing through the Grace Gate at Lord's, within earshot of frowning MCC members. Ironically, he's one of the two members of the side who is actually a member of the MCC.

His approach to batting is refreshingly simple, following the principle, 'if it's there, it's got to go'. Usually it does go, straight to the cover boundary, courtesy of the 'Chewton chop'. At our rare team meetings his contributions are equally forthright: he's not too concerned about the minutiae of the game; we have to 'get out there and fight and stuff 'em out of sight.'

He is everyone's favourite batting partner because of his unselfish running between the wickets and his stubborn refusal to give an inch, whatever the odds. He bats best when there is a crisis or a run-chase: he relishes a challenge and will never shirk it. He has often shepherded Somerset to victory in crucial one-day games (two brilliant Gillette Cup centuries against Surrey and Glamorgan spring to mind) and yet he has always recoiled from the limelight afterwards. Alan Gibson has recalled hearing a radio interview with Pete after he had played a match-winning innings for Somerset[13]:

The enthusiastic radio interviewer warmly congratulated him, at which Peter gave a polite grunt. The enthusiastic radio interviewer felt he was not

Away from cricket Brian enjoys the gentler pursuits of golf and gardening.

getting enough out of his subject, so pursued vigorously:

E.R.I.   Well, now, after this great, great performance today you'll be looking forward to greater, greater things.

P.W.D.   (Indistinguishable mutter.)

E.R.I.   D'you expect to be in the England side soon?

PWD.   Er, no.

E.R.I.   But why do you say that?

P.W.D.   Not good enough,

Collapse of interviewer who was unaccustomed to sportsmen disinclined to boast.

Almost as important as his contributions on the field is the fact that, if you're stuck in a dreary Northampton hotel looking for some company, you can always rely on Dash to be at the bar ready for a pint or two.

Pete Denning could only have played for Somerset. At first glance Brian Rose could have slotted into several county sides. He's more urbane and far more likely to get on a short list for a BBC newsreader. But this is a false impression. One of his greatest regrets is that *Wisden* records his birthplace as Dartford, Kent. In fact he passed only three weeks of his life there, having lived in Weston ever since. As a result, he has spent many hours explaining that he's definitely not a Somerset 'import'. He's still dismayed that Weston now falls into the boundaries of Avon. I've never met anyone who was proud to be born in Avon.

His career as a batsman has fallen into a familiar pattern amongst county cricketers. Initially he was an uninhibited stroke player specialising in booming straight drives. In 1972 he smashed 125, including 25 boundaries against Kent at Glastonbury – no doubt they wished that he'd remained in Dartford. When he returned from PE college in 1975 his game became more restricted: most of his runs were collected from deflections on the leg side. In effect, the innocence of youth had been replaced by the desire to establish himself as a reliable professional and, more importantly, a regular first team player. In 1978, his place secure (he was, after all, captain), the attacking strokes returned in abundance.

He played nine times for England and will admit to being a far superior player during his second spell in 1980 against the West Indies, when he topped the English batting averages. Eye trouble in the West Indies terminated his Test career prematurely. A mild, almost vague exterior hid an unexpected reservoir of courage and determination, as we were soon to discover in 1978.

So, early on the morning of Sunday, 5th September, 1976, the toll gates on the Severn Bridge were clicking incessantly as hordes of Somerset supporters poured into the Principality. Before 11 o'clock 5,000 West Countrymen had established themselves inside Sophia Gardens. Unfortunately for the Glamorgan treasurer there had been no gatemen to receive them. By one o'clock despairing Welsh officials were parading around the ground carrying buckets and pleading for their lost revenue. I hazard a guess that not everyone contributed.

A victory against lowly Glamorgan (16th in the John Player League) would be sufficient to ensure that elusive first trophy. Our supporters were buoyantly optimistic.

Close won the toss and, adopting the usual Sunday format, asked Glamorgan to bat. He recalls two fatal mistakes in the Glamorgan innings of 191. Close himself dropped the ageless Alan Jones and Malcolm Nash escaped being run out when stranded yards from home before he'd scored. In his autobiography, Close nobly refuses to name the offending fielder. Alan Jones went on to make 70, Nash 43.

In reply Somerset soon lost Denning, Close and Botham, and it was left to Kitchen (46) and Rose (39) to repair the innings. Then Burgess, batting at number six, led the charge, driving his 14-stone frame between the wickets with the desperation of an escaping prisoner of war; 31 runs were needed off four overs, ten off the last over, three (to tie and secure the title) off the last ball. Budgie heaved Nash to long on and both batsmen set off. Colin Dredge failed by less than a yard to complete the third run. Graham Burgess remained at the wicket 48 not out and exhausted, while the Welsh celebrated as if they themselves had won the League. Then slowly he dragged himself back to the pavilion. Since that day Somerset have not lost to Glamorgan in a one-day match.

A season's toil had gone unrewarded, the difference between success and failure being the length of a cricket bat. Next time would be even harder. Perhaps Somerset, everyone wondered, lacked the mettle to jump the final hurdle. Our failure to win a trophy was beginning to become a millstone around our necks. Of the other counties only Essex's cupboard remained bare. Northamptonshire had broken their duck the previous day in the Gillette Cup Final. Somerset, however, remained a Cinderella county.

At the end of the 1977 season Brian Close, aged 46, finally called it a day. In his last Championship game at Taunton he led a spirited and successful run-chase with Pete Denning (adding 144 in 91 minutes) against the 'old enemy', Gloucestershire – a happy memory for the Somerset faithful who had taken the 'Old Blighter' to their hearts.

Close had had a fustrating start to the season, being hampered by injury and loss of form. He had returned briefly at Bath to lead Somerset against the Australian touring side, but even then he had been compelled to watch the final day's play from the confines of the pavilion. Unable to check his natural exuberance, he had suffered a fall at the Roman Baths during a reception given to the tourists; he was in the process of breaking the world record for underwater swimming at the time. Not many 46 year-olds would have attempted it.

In superb weather, against the picturesque backcloth of Georgian Bath, Somerset trounced the Australians for the first time by seven wickets in a tremendous game of cricket. Greg Chappell, Brian Rose and David Hookes scored hundreds; Botham peppered the new sports centre with several straight sixes; Graham Burgess confused the visitors with his assortment of swingers; Thomson bowled 15 no-balls in seven overs as he grew increasingly infuriated by the 'Chewton chop' – a shot obviously foreign to Queensland – and Somerset's debutant opening bowler took 4 for 66. His name was Joel Garner, who was Littleborough's professional in the Lancashire League. He was to play three Championship matches in 1977, as well as the Gillette Cup games. Wouldn't it be a good idea, we all thought, if he could play regularly?

Close would have dearly loved to lead Somerset out at Lord's in the Gillette Cup Final in his last year, and his dream was nearly realised. Victories against Northumberland and Derbyshire took us to Lord's on 17th August for the semi-final; the match was finally completed on 26th August – it rained for a week. The initial three days were washed out and a championship match between the sides was postponed to try to fit in the tie. Eventually the umpires decided upon a match of 15 overs each. Mike Smith, Middlesex's acting captain, put Somerset in to bat. To quote *Wisden*: 'Somerset batted far more frantically than the situation warranted against bowling that would have tested even the most rational batting.'[14] We were dismissed for 59 and Middlesex achieved their target in the 12th over, despite Garner taking four wickets. The whole affair had proved to be an appalling anticlimax. A disillusioned Brian Close declared after the game: 'That's the story of my life – a complete farce.'

It is true that the last days of Brian Close's time at Somerset personified his career, for it remained sadly unfulfilled. Few players have had an international career spanning 27 years and yet played in only 18

Test matches. Moreover the fairy-tale ending to his career was snatched from him by the vagaries of the weather, resulting in an important semi-final being reduced to the format of a village beer match. Yet Brian Close is nothing if not resilient. Throughout his life he has had plenty of experience in coping with disappointment. He wrote after his retirement:

I very badly wanted to win something for Somerset, to repay a little to the county which had given me such a warm and sincere welcome when my cricket career seemed shattered. Unfortunately I failed in the end but we had fun – and a few near misses. I hope their memories of me are as warm as mine of Somerset and its cricket.[9]

Somerset v Australians at Bath, 18th, 19th and 20th May, 1977

AUSTRALIANS

First Innings		Second Innings	
R. B. McCosker, c Botham b Garner	2	run out	2
C. S. Sergeant, st Taylor b Burgess	13	c Garner b Botham	50
*G. S. Chappell, b Garner	113	c Garner b Botham	39
G. J. Cosier, b Garner	44	c Taylor b Botham	2
K. D. Walters, c Denning b Burgess	23	b Botham	25
D. W. Hookes, b Botham	3	b Burgess	108
†R. W. Marsh, b Garner	3	b Garner	0
K. J. O'Keeffe, c Denning b Burgess	11	c Denning b Moseley	20
J. R. Thomson, b Burgess	0	c Botham b Garner	0
M. F. Malone, b Burgess	2	c Richards b Breakwell	17
G. Dymock, not out	0	not out	6
Extras (b 10, w 2, n-b 6)	18	Extras (b 4, l-b 10, w 1, n-b 5)	20
	232		289

Fall of wickets: 1/2, 2/57, 3/177, 4/197, 5/200, 6/204, 7/223, 8/223, 9/231.

1/16, 2/18, 3/141, 4/172, 5/183, 6/214, 7/251, 8/252, 9/271.

Bowling: *First Innings:* Garner 20–8–66–4; Moseley 16–5–52–0; Burgess 9.3–2–25–5; Botham 15–2–48–1; Breakwell 7–0–23–0.

Second Innings: Garner 23–6–71–2; Moseley 17–6–55–1; Botham 22–6–98–4; Burgess 9–3–41–1; Breakwell 0.3–0–4–1.

SOMERSET

First Innings		Second Innings	
B. C. Rose, not out	110	c Marsh b Thomson	27
P. W. Denning, c Marsh b Dymock	39	b Chappell	34
I. V. A. Richards, c Hookes b Malone	18	c Cosier b O'Keeffe	53
*D. B. Close, c McCosker b Malone	0		
D. Breakwell, c Chappell b O'Keeffe	23		
I. T. Botham, c McCosker b O'Keeffe	59	not out	39
P. A. Slocombe, not out	55	not out	8
G. I. Burgess,			
†D. J. S. Taylor,			
J. Garner,			
H. R. Moseley,			
Extras (b 4, l-b 6, n-b 26)	36	Extras (b 4, l-b 3, w 3, n-b 11)	21
5 wickets declared	340	3 wickets	182

Fall of wickets: 1/81, 2/116, 3/117, 4/146, 5/228.

1/50, 2/129, 3/129.

Bowling: *First Innings:* Thomson 16–2–60–0; Dymock 17–7–48–1; Malone 22–4–70–2; O'Keeffe 35–15–114–2; Chappell 2–0–11–0; Walters 2–1–1–0.

Second Innings: Thomson 12–1–57–1; Malone 9–2–18–0; Chappell 8–4–29–1; Dymock 5–0–25–0; O'Keeffe 5.1–0–32–1.

Somerset won by 7 wickets

6. 1978

It was not obvious who would replace Close. His successor would have an enormous task, since captaining a county cricket club is possibly the most arduous job in sport (Bobby Robson might disagree). The captain has such broad areas of responsibility: he has to organise pre-season training, to act as a buffer between the players and the committee, to be responsible for discipline; he has the most important role in deciding the selection for matches and the playing staff for seasons. Somehow he has to keep 18 players aiming for the same goals when only eleven can play at once; he's usually the player's mouthpiece to the press and often the press's scapegoat. When he's done all that, he must lead his side out onto the field in the most tactically exacting team game that's been devised – and he should score a few runs or take wickets as well. No wonder the casualty rate of county captains is high. Cricket managers can sometimes ease the burden, but their influence is invariably limited. I notice that Yorkshire have been more successful recently when Ray Illingworth has been on the field rather than in his office. The fact that Illingworth opted to play at all emphasises the point.

There were three major candidates for the post. Derek Taylor had deputised for Close on numerous occasions, his methodical common sense providing a ballast for Close's more instinctive methods. He could be relied upon to do a sensible, conscientious job, but his benefit year was coming up – always a hectic time – and perhaps he was too cautious and unambitious to drive the Somerset team to the limits of its potential. Peter Denning, universally respected by the players, had some experience of captaincy with youth sides and at St Luke's College, Exeter. The committee, however, chose Brian Rose, a brave decision since no one could quite predict how he would react to the challenge.

Early in his career he'd been nicknamed 'Dozy Rosey' – events sometimes seemed to pass him by, unnoticed. He tended to withdraw from dressing-room arguments and keep his own counsel. No one was quite sure what he was thinking, or whether he was thinking at all! So there was more speculation than usual when players reported for duty in April, 1978.

Rose was a revelation. He didn't suddenly become a domineering extrovert, but his quietly spoken words carried immense authority; he was not worried that he was younger or less famous than some of his teammates. It was clear that he had given much thought to the 1978 season. He wanted us to become meaner and more professional on the field and to disown our reputation for being colourful, unreliable crowd-pleasers. It was more important to win games. He had an eager audience: too many titles had already been snatched from our fingertips and his young side was just as hungry as he for success. Pre-season training was more organised and more rigorous than usual (fortunately I had disappeared to Oxford by this time).

Once the season started, the likes of Colin Dredge, Keith Jennings and Dennis Breakwell were given more responsibility and they responded readily, perhaps because their captain was no longer a legend in his own lifetime, but one of their contemporaries. Opposition sides also noticed a change. Somerset were far more miserly in the field and more unsmiling: incoming batsmen were not made to feel welcome at the wicket.

By 16th June Somerset were at the top of the Championship table, had reached the semi-final of the Benson & Hedges competition and were in contention for the John Player League. From now on every day's cricket was vital: there was no respite. It became a standing joke that, before each match, Brian Rose would declare, 'This is the most important match in the club's history.'

The first setback came in the Benson & Hedges semi-final against Kent at Taunton, in a match that took three days to complete. On a wicket that deteriorated considerably, Somerset failed by 41 runs to reach Kent's total of 204, despite valiant efforts from the 'old firm', Rose & Denning.

On 5th July the Gillette Cup competition began, Somerset meeting Warwickshire at Taunton. I was surprised to be selected, having just returned from University with only one game against the New Zealanders under my belt. Clearly Rose was putting his faith in the youngsters; neither Kitchen nor Burgess was selected.

The Warwickshire innings never lost its momentum and after 60 overs they had amassed a formidable 292 for 5. My eight overs were particularly expensive, a seething county ground proving a stark contrast to

Dennis Breakwell and myself are relieved after our John Player League win over Kent. (Somerset County Gazette).

(Below) Gillette Cup Final v Sussex. The tension shows on the faces of Pete Denning and Keith Jennings. (Somerset County Gazette).

Somerset players celebrate after their semi-final against Essex. (Somerset County Gazette).

the tranquil surroundings of the Parks. Somerset required the largest total, batting second, in the history of the competition.

Rose went early leg-before to David Brown; in the next 24 overs Denning and Richards added 137 before Dasher was bowled by Willis. By now the cramped viewing box next to the old pavilion was as crowded as a rush-hour tube train. There we calculated that we needed 140 in 28 overs, a target we would fancy in a John Player League game. The realisation grew that this massive total was attainable, especially if Viv stayed in. Peter Roebuck joined him and played brilliantly for 45, scoring at the same pace as Viv. Pete appreciated that if he played quietly, trying to give his partner the bowling, the pressure on Viv to do something extravagant, with the field deep set, would increase. So he decided to seize the initiative himself: 96 was added in 17 overs and Warwickshire were hamstrung. When Botham replaced Roebuck 43 were needed off 12 overs and only

a startling collapse (not unknown in Somerset cricket circles) could stop us winning.

Off the first ball of the 58th over Richards allowed himself the luxury of strolling down the wicket to Brown to hammer the ball high over the pavilion to win the match. Richards had produced the innings of a lifetime – at least for most mortals. Viv was to reach such heights for us on many occasions in the future.

In the next round at Cardiff the run glut continued, Somerset amassing 330 for 4, with Pete Denning scoring a magnificent 145. Joel Garner bowled his first six overs for five runs and one wicket and wasn't required again. Next, to Canterbury and a tense, low-scoring contest against Kent. Here Colin Dredge was the matchwinner, taking 4 for 23, including the vital wickets of Woolmer and Asif. During our innings we welcomed into our dressing room the Bishop of Bath and Wells, who was in Canterbury on business. Brian Rose politely introduced him to the members of the side present – after all, we needed all the help we could get. Keith Jennings, oblivious of the cricket as well as our distinguished visitor, was buried in a

WARWICKSHIRE

D. L. Amiss, c Dredge b Breakwell		70
K. D. Smith, c Rose b Breakwell		28
R. N. Abberley, c Botham b Garner		16
*J. Whitehouse, c sub b Dredge		94
†G. W. Humpage, b Botham		58
P. R. Oliver, not out		6
T. A. Lloyd, not out		8
E. E. Hemmings,		
D. J. Brown,		
R. G. D. Willis,		
S. P. Perryman,		
Extras (l-b 5, n-b 7)		12
	5 wickets 60 overs	292

Fall of wickets: 1/91, 2/118, 3/128, 4/278, 5/279.

Bowling: Garner 12–1–47–1; Botham 12–2–37–1; Dredge 10–0–58–1; Jennings 6–1–35–0; Breakwell 12–1–51–2; Marks 8–0–52–0.

SOMERSET

*B. C. Rose, lbw b Brown		11
P. W. Denning, b Willis		60
I. V. A. Richards, not out		139
P. M. Roebuck, c and b Perryman		45
I. T. Botham, c Brown b Hemmings		11
V. J. Marks, not out		15
D. Breakwell,		
†D. J. S. Taylor,		
J. Garner,		
K. F. Jennings,		
C. H. Dredge,		
Extras (b 6, l-b 6, w 1, n-b 3)		16
	4 wickets 57.1 overs	297

Fall of wickets: 1/17, 2/154, 3/250, 4/263.

Bowling: Willis 12–2–43–1; Brown 11.1–0–54–1; Perryman 12–0–56–1; Oliver 11–0–70–0; Hemmings 11–0–58–1.

Somerset won by 6 wickets

---

magazine of a distinctly unecclesiastical nature. When Brian introduced Keith to his guest I can report that the Bishop hid any embarrassment far more effectively than the speechless Somerset medium pacer. Anyway there was no divine retribution forthcoming that day, as we won by five wickets.

Somerset were rewarded with a home draw against Essex in the semi-final on 18th August. By 10.30 the ground was packed and the gates were locked until Chairman Herbie Hoskins decided to reopen them. Denning failed a fitness test and was replaced by Phil Slocombe – I've always been grateful that I've never had to undergo a fitness test as I'm sure I'd fail it, whether injured or not.

Rose elected to bat and soon lost his partner in Norbert Phillip's first over. Richards came in and began where he'd left off against Warwickshire; balls outside the off stump were whipped through mid-wicket without the semblance of risk. Rose was more subdued, playing five consecutive maidens from Stuart Turner; eventually he lost patience and holed out at mid off. Roebuck again made an important contribution, adding 103 with Richards, who was at his flamboyant best. Stepping away to the leg side, he smashed left arm spinner Ray East over the extra cover boundary and into the organ works – a shot that left everyone gasping. Finally he was brilliantly caught by Denness off a full blooded drive, for a breathtaking 116. The last ten overs produced 79 runs and our total of 287 was sufficient to generate considerable optimism in our dressing room. But always in the back of our minds was the memory of the Warwickhire match. If two batsmen are set, Taunton can seem impossible to defend with its fast outfield and short straight boundaries.

After losing Denness in the second over Essex advanced steadily. Whenever a wicket fell the new batsman seemed immediately able to maintain the momentum of their innings. Gooch flexed his blacksmith's forearms, Fletcher improvised delicately, McEwan drove imperiously. At 246–4 the situation was desperate, whereupon Botham entered the fray, first by brilliantly running out Keith Pont and then by catching Keith Fletcher off his own bowling. Next Phillip suffered an extremely rare and unfortunate dismissal, run out by Marks! Suddenly it was 248–7. We had some breathing space at last, although not for long.

Turner struck two consecutive boundaries off Botham; 23 were needed off three overs when Ian got his revenge, clean bowling him. Garner bowled his final over cheaply, leaving Colin Dredge to bowl the

SOMERSET		
*B. C. Rose, c East b Pont		24
P. A. Slocombe, lbw b Phillip		0
I. V. A. Richards, c Denness b Gooch		116
P. M. Roebuck, c Lever b Phillip		57
I. T. Botham, b East		7
V. J. Marks, not out		33
G. I. Burgess, b Lever		5
D. Breakwell, not out		17
†D. J. S. Taylor,		
J. Garner,		
C. H. Dredge,		
Extras (b 10, l-b 14, w 1, n-b 3)		28
6 wickets 60 overs		287

Fall of wickets: 1/2, 2/86, 3/189, 4/208, 5/247, 6/255.
Bowling: Lever 12–0–61–1; Phillip 11–1–56–2; Turner 8–6–22–0; Pont 6–1–35–1; Gooch 12–0–42–1; East 11–1–43–1.

ESSEX		
M. H. Denness, c Marks b Dredge		3
G. A. Gooch, c Taylor b Garner		61
K. S. McEwan, b Burgess		37
*K. W. R. Fletcher, c and b Botham		67
B. R. Hardie, run out		21
K. R. Pont, run out		39
N. Phillip, run out		1
S. Turner, b Botham		12
R. E. East, b Dredge		10
†N. Smith, run out		6
J. K. Lever, not out		5
Extras (b 14, l-b 9, n-b 2)		25
60 overs		287

Fall of wickets: 1/9, 2/70, 3/127, 4/166, 5/246, 6/248, 7/248, 8/266, 9/281.
Bowling: Garner 12–1–46–1; Dredge 12–0–60–2; Botham 12–1–48–2; Burgess 12–1–43–1; Breakwell 2–0–11–0; Marks 1–0–13–0; Richards 9–1–41–0.

Somerset won with the scores level, having lost fewer
wickets

---

sixtieth, Essex needing 12 to win with two wickets in hand.

The first ball went for a single, the second for four, but the third knocked back Ray East's middle stump. The fourth to Lever was a disaster: a no-ball followed by overthrows – three runs accrued: Somerset appeared to be labouring under a death wish. Four runs needed off three balls: Essex favourites again. At the next ball, Smith swung and missed: Somerset favourites. Off the sixth ball, one run. Three needed off the last ball. I was at deep mid wicket, a prime area for the late order batsmen to seek, praying that the ball would go elsewhere; I knew that this was not the sort of attitude that should be adopted by professional sportsmen but I could see several others offering identical prayers.

Fittingly the ball sped to the captain at deep point. He lost it for a while amidst the scurrying white bodies in the distance. Eventually he located it and sent it back to Taylor who dived at the stumps. The Essex wicket-keeper, Smith, was two feet short of a Gillette Cup Final appearance.

Afterwards everyone collapsed for a while. Even the crowd was subdued – they were exhausted too. My wife, not one of the world's most ardent cricket enthusiasts, declared that she'd been fascinated as much by the crowd's reactions to the game as by the game itself. I think she was in a minority. A number of Essex players gallantly entered our dressing room to share some champagne. Everyone was in a state of shock, slowly trying to assemble in their minds the proceedings of the last eight hours. Gradually it sank in: we were in the Gillette Cup Final.

In between the feverish excitement of the Gillette Cup matches we maintained our interest in the Championship until late August when defeat against Middlesex ruled out the possibility of overhauling Kent and Essex. Our involvement in all four domestic competitions had begun to take its toll. In the end we were to finish a respectable fourth with nine victories to our credit.

In the John Player League nine consecutive wins had taken us to the top of the table. Seven of these victories had been gained batting second. The policy was to insert the opposition if the toss was won,

At 10.15 the dressing room is still busy as Somerset players try to work out how we reached the finals. I think the magnum of champagne is probably empty by the look of Peter Roebuck. (Somerset County Gazette).

preferring to put our faith in our batsmen when the pressure was greatest, in the final stages of the match. Moreover if rain intervened, the advantage would invariably lie with the side batting last.

All was to be decided on the weekend of September 2nd and 3rd. On the Saturday we were to meet Sussex at Lord's, on Sunday, Essex at Taunton. After 103 years Somerset had the chance to win not one, but two trophies within 48 hours.

The week before the final was hectic and full of new experiences. HTV cameras popped up everywhere to make a documentary and we all enjoyed the novelty of their attention: I fear that we spent much of the time trying to sabotage their efforts. We chartered two seven-seater aircraft to fly to Scarborough to fulfil our commitments in the Fenner Trophy. Scrambled arrangements were made to get countless friends and relatives inside Lord's on Saturday. All of Somerset was talking about the coming weekend and

this time the mood was expectant rather than hopeful. After the drama of previous games, the escapes from desperate situations, this had to be Somerset's year. The papers made us favourites for both competitions. Even *The Times* thundered in our favour, John Woodcock writing, 'Somerset have never won the County Championship nor in the 15 years since they started, any of the one-day competitions. By tomorrow night they should have won two.'[15]

Unfortunately not even *The Times* is infallible nowadays. At Lord's we played abysmally. Only Rose, Richards and Botham made significant contributions in our total of 207. Richards, as if carrying the burden of the whole side on his shoulders, scored a subdued 44. Only Botham, with a belligerent 80, batted with his normal freedom. In reply the Sussex openers Barclay and Mendis withstood the opening burst from Garner and Botham, adding 93 for the first wicket. Despite a hiccough in the middle of their innings Sussex sailed home by five wickets with seven overs to spare.

Why, after all the brave deeds earlier in the year, did we perform so tepidly in the final? We might

SOMERSET		
*B. C. Rose, c Long b Cheatle		30
P. W. Denning, b Imran		0
I. V. A. Richards, c Arnold b Barclay		44
P. M. Roebuck, c Mendis b Cheatle		9
I. T. Botham, b Imran		80
V. J. Marks, c Arnold b Barclay		4
G. I. Burgess, run out		3
†D. J. S. Taylor, not out		13
J. Garner, not out		8
K. F. Jennings,		
C. H. Dredge,		
Extras (l-b 10, n-b 6)		16
	7 wickets 60 overs	207

Fall of wickets: 1/22, 2/53, 3/73, 4/115, 5/151, 6/157, 7/194.

Bowling: Imran 12-1-50-2; Arnold 12-2-43-0; Spencer 12-3-27-0; Cheatle 12-3-50-2; Barclay 12-3-21-2.

SUSSEX		
J. R. T. Barclay, c Roebuck b Botham		44
G. D. Mendis, c Marks b Burgess		44
P. W. G. Parker, not out		62
Javed Miandad, c Taylor b Garner		0
Imran Khan, c and b Botham		3
C. P. Phillipson, c Taylor b Dredge		32
S. J. Storey, not out		0
*†A. Long,		
J. Spencer,		
G. G. Arnold,		
R. G. L. Cheatle,		
Extras (b 1, l-b 9, w 7, n-b 9)		26
	5 wickets 53.1 overs	211

Fall of wickets: 1/93, 2/106, 3/106, 4/110, 5/207.

Bowling: Garner 12-3-34-1; Dredge 10-2-26-1; Botham 12-1-65-2; Jennings 9-1-29-0; Burgess 10-2-27-1; Denning 0.1-0-4-0.

Sussex won by 5 wickets

10.15. Viv and Ian locked in conversation with Roy Kerslake and Brian Langford. (Somerset County Gazette).

claim to be exhausted after such a gruelling season, but the adrenalin created by a Lord's final should have overcome that. In simple terms, we lost our nerve: we were intimidated by the occasion. In recent years we have witnessed the paralysing effect of a capacity Lord's ground. Surrey and Nottinghamshire batsmen in the Benson & Hedges finals in 1981 and 1982 have emerged from the pavilion with pale, dazed faces, unlikely to achieve anything. In 1978 we were the same: we were so worried about losing the game that we were frightened to seize the initiative and win it. Fear of failure is the most destructive element in professional sport. One of the reasons that Ian Botham has achieved so much is the fact that he is courageous enough to risk looking a complete idiot. He allows himself to explore the extreme limits of his talents rather than settling for safe mediocrity.

Pehaps I should add that Sussex played quite well on the day, too.

The next day the county ground at Taunton was packed, yet again. Essex, no doubt mindful of their experiences two weeks before, were determined to provide stern opposition. There was one team change: I was omitted in favour of Phil Slocombe. The crowd cheered as they learned that Essex would bat.

At first everything went according to plan; the previous day's disappointments seemed to be shelved. After 29 overs Essex had stumbled to 92 for 4. Thereafter there was chaos – Fletcher, Pont and Hardie plundered 98 off the final 11 overs, leaving a target of 190. Our spirits had been dented by the mayhem of the closing overs. After a poor start Richards, Roebuck, Botham and Slocombe took us to 157 for 7 from 36 overs. It was agonising to watch. After his dismissal Pete Roebuck chose to wander around a deserted Taunton. He recalls:

I could not possibly watch those death throes . . . It was beautifully tranquil in the streets with scarcely anyone about at all. A few swans wandered down the Tone undisturbed by muffled roars a few hundred yards away. A few families pottered around on their Sunday outing blissfully unaware of events at the County Ground.

It was a lovely day. I'd not noticed before.[4]

Watching from the 'box' was intolerable. As ever, the tension was worst for those not actively involved, such as Roy Kerslake, our long-suffering cricket chairman, and Jock McCombe. I decided to witness the last rites from the top of the indoor school, prowling up and down the roof, hoping for some mighty blow into the graveyard. I looked down upon 10,000 Somerset folk willing us to win. In the middle

Joel's expression suggests that the Essex win was too close for comfort. (Somerset County Gazette).

Keith Jennings, more red-faced than ever, was swinging desperately and scampering singles. But boundaries were needed. Every Essex fielder was patrolling the outfield, forming an impenetrable screen. Four were needed off the last ball. Jennings heaved and ran but all to no avail.

I returned to our dressing room. There was complete silence, just bodies slumped dejectedly on chairs and benches. There was nothing to say, no post mortems, or recriminations, no vain attempts to raise our spirits. Outside, the thousands, who had supported us all season, massed around the pavilion, cheering and calling for their players. We were persuaded reluctantly to go up to the viewing box to pay our respects to them. The reception we received was overwhelming and heightened our sorrow. We felt that we had let them down: but they didn't seem to mind; they stayed behind chanting incessantly as if expressing their forgiveness as well as their gratitude. The crowd's reaction to our second defeat had a deep effect on us all. Tears quietly flowed down the cheeks of several players as we went back to the dressing room. Still no one spoke. Eventually the silence was broken. Viv Richards, as committed to Somerset cricket as any man from Stogumber or Norton Fitzwarren, withdrew to the bathroom with his treasured Stuart Surridge Jumbo and smashed it into little pieces.

Somerset v Essex, John Player League
3rd September, 1978

ESSEX

A. W. Lilley, c Denning b Burgess	13
G. A. Gooch, c Burgess b Botham	7
K. S. McEwan, b Moseley	2
*K. W. R. Fletcher, not out	76
K. R. Pont, b Dredge	35
B. R. Hardie, b Botham	38
N. Phillip,	
S. Turner,	
R. E. East,	
†N. Smith,	
J. K. Lever,	
Extras (l-b 16, n-b 3)	19
5 wickets 40 overs	190

Fall of wickets: 1/16, 2/25, 3/29, 4/92, 5/190.
Bowling: Botham 8–0–38–2; Moseley 8–0–20–1; Burgess 8–0–20–1; Jennings 8–0–38–0; Dredge 8–0–55–1.

SOMERSET

*B. C. Rose, b Lever	9
P. W. Denning, c Smith b Phillip	8
I. V. A. Richards, c Hardie b Gooch	26
P. M. Roebuck, b East	30
I. T. Botham, c McEwan b Phillip	45
P. A. Slocombe, b Lever	20
G. I. Burgess, c and b Turner	0
K. F. Jennings, not out	14
C. H. Dredge, b Lever	14
†D. J. S. Taylor, run out	4
H. R. Moseley, run out	0
Extras (b 2, l-b 12, w 1, n-b 3)	18
40 overs	188

Fall of wickets: 1/18, 2/18, 3/69, 4/87, 5/139, 6/140, 7/157, 8/177, 9/185.
Bowling: Lever 8–0–38–3; Phillip 8–0–35–2; Gooch 8–0–31–1; Turner 8–0–32–1; East 8–0–34–1.

Essex won by 2 runs

This team photo was taken before the semi-final. Dasher looks suitably grumpy having just failed a fitness test. (Somerset County Gazette).

7. 1979

By April, 1979, we were all talking again. Indeed there was plenty to talk about. Ian Botham had just returned from England's triumphant tour against a Packer-torn Australian side. Meanwhile Viv had been smashing their first team around various strange venues in Sydney and Melbourne. Pete Roebuck had spent his winter teaching at Cranbrook School in the pleasant suburbs of Sydney, enjoying the surf on Bondi beach. I'd been doing a similar job but in the slightly less idyllic surroundings of Tiverton, Devon. Pete Denning, we were informed, was now an expert in the demolition trade. Colin Dredge had been scoring goals for Frome, whilst Keith Jennings would lay aside his hammer and chisel at the weekends to score tries and sink pints on behalf of Wiveliscombe Rugby Club. Derek Taylor, having sold all his Christmas cards, had been busy preparing for his benefit year.

At the beginning of a season everyone is pleased to see each other. Topics of conversation range from the form of Tottenham Hotspur and Scunthorpe United to Mrs Thatcher's latest round of spending cuts and the Dredges' latest offspring. Eventually our minds turn to cricket and the forthcoming season.

We felt that we had learnt much from the 1978 season. We appreciated how much hard graft was required to get into a position where we could actually win titles. In 1978 we had squandered our chances; we realized that it would take a tremendous effort to create the same opportunities again. Hundreds of county cricketers play out their careers without ever winning a medal or appearing in a Lord's final, but we were fed up with being gallant losers. Already there was a deep determination to atone for the acute disappointments of the 1978 season.

This determination was reflected in a little incident at Worcester. In the final Benson & Hedges zonal match, Rose declared our innings closed with the score at 1 for 0 wicket, thereby ensuring, so we thought, our place in the quarter finals. The 100 paying spectators were aghast and then outraged. The slide rule had banished us to second place in the John Player League in 1976 and 1978, so we thought that we would use it to our advantage this time. Not everyone was impressed by Somerset's declaration, though I'm sure the Worcestershire players were

quite happy about it and so were the sports editors. As the rain continued to pour down, thereby depriving cricket correspondents around the country of any action to report, the 'Worcester affair' dominated the sports pages for a week.

Donald Carr, the Secretary of the TCCB, declared, 'Somerset's action is totally contrary to the spirit of the competition, but is not in breach of the rules as they are written.' An inquiry would be held at the end of the season. Letters flooded into the offices of Fleet Street as well as the county ground, most, though not all, condemning Somerset's action. Some surmised that W.G., no doubt taking guard on some Elysian cricket field, was hiding a wry grin beneath his bushy beard. Special meetings of the TCCB were called at Lord's and within a week Somerset were banned from the competition.

Throughout the week the Somerset players remained tightlipped. Unfortunately we were marooned in hotel rooms most of the time, unable to vent our feelings on the wife or the dog, or even in the middle, for the rain continued to fall. In such circumstances it is possible to lose all sense of proportion. We felt branded as criminals and it seemed as if we would never be allowed to forget 24th May. There had been a suggestion in the press that we might have placed bets on Worcester winning the game. That made everyone very angry. The declaration had been made purely in the interests of Somerset cricket: it had also revealed to everyone our desperation to win a trophy.

Brian Rose had been shattered by the whole affair and was even contemplating resignation. The big question for us, and for Brian in particular, was, how would our supporters react? We found out on 3rd June – a John Player League game at Taunton against Hampshire. Brian recalls the match:

Before the start of the game, Somerset's players, myself in particular, were apprehensive about the kind of reception we would be given in the wake of the Worcester controversy, even though we had received hundreds of good luck messages. I don't think any of us expected such a welcoming roar as the one which greeted us when we stepped out onto the pitch.[16]

Budgie bows out with a glass of champagne.

Inevitably we won that game and Rose, run out for 25, was given the sort of ovation that is usually reserved for Test centurions at Lord's. The whole affair, allied to the crowd's reaction, strengthened our resolve to win something.

Our progress in the Championship was restricted by poor weather, the World Cup, which deprived us of our three 'superstars' for three weeks, and sixteen draws. Ironically, since the arrival of Richards we have won very few run-chases in the Championship, as opposition captains start making their calculations on the assumption that Viv will score a hundred in eighty minutes. We lost just one game – the final one against Sussex under extenuating circumstances – thus ending the longest unbeaten run in the club's history (23 matches).

In the John Player League we managed to win both games during the World Cup, beating Gloucestershire by eight wickets and Essex by nine, just to prove that it was possible for Somerset to triumph without Richards, Garner and Botham. Yet again it

was impossible to settle down to a plateful of roast beef and Yorkshire pudding at Sunday lunchtime without a few butterflies ruining my appetite.

After a bye in the first round of the Gillette Cup we entertained Derbyshire at Taunton, beating them by eight wickets thanks to fine batting from Rose, Slocombe and Richards, which brought Kent down the M5 for the quarter final on 8th August. Already Essex had won the Benson & Hedges competition and were virtually assured of the Championship pennant. There remained just one county without a title to its credit.

The Kent game provided another remarkable contest for the Taunton crowd to savour. Somerset were reduced to 45 for 4, whereupon Richards and Botham sparkled briefly, adding 50 in eleven overs. But by lunch they had both gone; the score was 112 for 7 and as I delivered the salads there was an air of despondency in the dressing room. Soon after lunch we slumped to 126 for 8. Graham Burgess had taken root at one end but no one appeared able to stay with him – we would settle for 150. Garner played with unusual caution, whilst Burgess slowly found his touch. Budgie was summoning up all his years of experience now – he would trust his partners and try to bat the sixty overs rather than die in a blaze of glory. Garner eventually lost patience at 157; he didn't bother to hide his annoyance as he walloped his thigh and cast his eyes to the heavens as if seeking forgiveness.

Keith Jennings was our last batsman. He always looked a polished player but rarely scored any runs. Keith blocked furiously as Budgie picked up singles, interspersed by the occasional late cut off Underwood. They continued to frustrate the Kent bowlers until the second ball of the sixtieth over when Jennings was bowled by John Shepherd. The last two wickets had added 64 crucial runs. Budgie received a standing ovation, having scored 50 in 35 overs.

In contrast to the gloom of lunchtime, the atmosphere in the dressing room was now buoyant. 190 had been beyond our expectations; we had given ourselves a chance to win. There followed one of the most inspired spells of out cricket that I've ever witnessed.

Garner was in devastating form; Ian Botham took two staggering catches at second slip, Taylor two excellent ones behind the stumps. The crowd quickly caught the mood of the players; as our opening bowlers hurtled up to the wickets, one like an enraged bull, the other a galloping giraffe, they opened their throats and roared. By the time Botham and Garner were rested Kent were 40 for 5. Jennings and Burgess replaced them and maintained the pressure; Breakwell hung onto a skier and by tea Kent were 59 for 7. Afterwards Garner and Botham were summoned for mopping up operations and Kent were dismissed for 60 in the 29th over.

Unsurprisingly Garner (5 for 11) was made man of the match. Yet I wonder if Somerset would have

---

Somerset v Kent, Gillette Cup Quarter Final
8th August, 1979

SOMERSET

*B. C. Rose, c Downton b Dilley	15
P. A. Slocombe, c Tavaré b Dilley	2
I. V. A. Richards, c Downton b Woolmer	44
P. M. Roebuck, c Downton b Jarvis	6
P. W. Denning, c Tavaré b Woolmer	3
I. T. Botham, c Underwood b Woolmer	29
G. I. Burgess, not out	50
D. Breakwell, c Tavaré b Woolmer	8
†D. J. S. Taylor, c Downton b Shepherd	2
J. Garner, b Asif	12
K. F. Jennings, b Shepherd	7
Extras (b 1, l-b 6, w 1, n-b 4)	12
59.2 overs	190

Fall of wickets: 1/16, 2/21, 3/33, 4/45, 5/95, 6/102, 7/110, 8/126, 9/157.

Bowling: Jarvis 11–1–40–1; Dilley 12–3–28–2; Woolmer 12–2–28–4; Shepherd 10.2–2–41–2; Underwood 9–4–26–0; Asif 5–0–15–1.

KENT

R. A. Woolmer, c Botham b Garner	6
G. W. Johnson, b Garner	1
C. J. Tavaré, c Taylor b Garner	0
Asif Iqbal, b Botham	10
*A. G. E. Ealham, b Garner	0
J. N. Shepherd, c Botham b Jennings	9
C. S. Cowdrey, c Breakwell b Burgess	12
†P. R. Downton, b Garner	6
G. R. Dilley, lbw b Botham	0
D. L. Underwood, c Taylor b Botham	0
K. B. S. Jarvis, not out	0
Extras (l-b 5, w 1, n-b 10)	16
28.4 overs	60

Fall of wickets: 1/14, 2/14, 3/17, 4/19, 5/40, 6/54, 7/59, 8/60, 9/60.

Bowling: Garner 9.4–2–11–5; Botham 10–4–15–3; Burgess 5–3–12–1; Jennings 4–2–6–1.

Somerset won by 130 runs

---

taken the field in such a positive frame of mind if it hadn't been for the innings of Graham Burgess. His performance had opened up the possibility of victory in the team's mind. It was as if Budgie, while batting, had seen his last chance of a medal slipping away after fourteen years of yeoman service. He was the only survivor of the 1967 Gillette final and this was to be his final year.

Graham Burgess had joined the staff in 1966 at the age of 23. He regrets Somerset's reluctance to take him on earlier as he was compelled to assert himself on the first team at an age when his contemporaries, Roy Virgin and Mervyn Kitchen, were already established members of the side.

Unlike some professional cricketers, Budgie loved cricket. In fact he liked talking and thinking about the game almost as much as playing. He would purr with delight at a Richards (I.V.A.) on drive or a Richards (B.A.) cover drive. Stored away in the back of his mind was a file of opposition batsmen's strengths and weaknesses. Many times have we heard Budgie's reassuring words: X 'is a fine player – with good arms – but he can't play the inswinger.'

He was a brilliant all-round sportsman. Peter Roebuck recalls: 'He used to sit in a chair to play table tennis (itself an insight into his abilities and failings!) and still hammer all-comers.'[4] Despite his bulk he was a touch player. I think he gained far greater satisfaction from a delicate late cut trickling to the third man boundary than blasting the ball into the churchyard. At his best he was a delight to watch. Yet his record as a batsman does not match his natural sense of timing (career batting average of 19). Perhaps this was because he always strove for perfection rather than simply relying on his natural ability as a hitter.

Nor did his bowling depend upon his undoubted strength. He preferred to use cunning and deceit as a medium pace swing bowler rather than trying to knock people's helmets off – that was far too strenuous anyway. It was fascinating to field at mid-on during a Burgess spell. Invariably he would begin with a no-ball as he strove for his rhythm. Thereafter he would start plotting. I would watch which side the shiny part of the ball was held: perhaps he would deliver an over of inswingers; then I'd notice the slightly different grip and the twinkle in his eye. Off he trotted with the away swinger. If it worked the unsuspecting batsman might be bowled or caught behind and Budgie would beam modestly, happy in his craft. If it didn't and the ball disappeared through square leg, he'd shrug his shoulders, smile and explain that it didn't swing. Then we'd share another mint.

When he retired to take up a coaching post at

Monmouth School we missed his contributions with bat and ball in one-day cricket, his hearty laugh and his self-deprecating sense of humour. He still pops over the bridge now and again to watch us and we're never surprised to see him – he loves the game too much to stay away for long.

In the semi-final at Lord's we were again indebted to Burgess, this time in his role as a bowler. He took 3 for 25 from his twelve overs and, along with Joel Garner, helped restrict Middlesex to 185. Peter Denning was the mainstay of Somerset's reply, batting throughout the innings for a splendid 90. No matter how many men Brearley posted at third man and square cover, Pete still found the gaps. Botham ended the match with a six off the second ball he received, with ten overs to spare.

So we found ourselves in an almost identical situation to 1978, the only difference being that we had to rely upon Middlesex beating Kent at Canterbury to give us a chance of the John Player League title. The week before the final was less frantic than in 1978: there were no camera crews or flights to Scarborough but two three-day matches to distract our minds. In the second, against Sussex, with Rose, Richards and Garner resting, we lost our season's unbeaten record in the Championship.

Not too dismayed, we packed our bags and travelled from Hove to the Europa Hotel in Grosvenor Square. After a sumptuous team dinner most of us headed for our bedrooms – through choice rather than compulsion. Curfews have rarely been imposed on Somerset players during my time at the club. At Northampton in 1976 it was tried and on the following day Roy Virgin (145) and Peter Willey (227*) added 370 out of a total of 482 for 6. The match was lost by an innings and 86 runs and the experiment was never repeated. Each player learns how to prepare himself best before a big game – Joel Garner, for instance, prefers to sleep soundly for five hours rather than toss and turn for nine. Most of us indulged in several glasses of wine to combat insomnia. Brian Rose, who reckons that he slept for just 45 minutes the night before the Sussex final, slept like a baby. I adjourned with my trusty room mate Peter Roebuck to discuss the implications of Plato's Theory of Forms for modern society – or did we dwell on Sarfraz's inswinger? I can't remember.

In the morning the sun was shining and the ground full. Rose lost the toss and was glad. Our inclination

The Gillette Cup is ours and Brian Rose can scarcely believe it. (Somerset County Gazette).

had been to insert the opposition, sticking to the trusted formula; psychologically we preferred batting second. But it was an ideal day for batting first with little cloud or overnight dew. Jim Watts chose to field.

Rose and Denning began swiftly, adding 34 runs before Denning was caught behind off Sarfraz. Richards then entered his stage and played an innings of masterful control. He recalls his thoughts before going to the crease: 'I willed myself until it physically hurt. There must be nothing ruthless or irresponsible. It wasn't a day for daring, carefree sixes.'[11] In a chanceless innings he batted from the seventh to the sixtieth over. You can never be certain that Richards is going to score a century in a Lord's final, but what you do know is that he's the most likely man in the world to do so. His ability to score runs when it really matters is what separates him from the other great players in the world. Towards the end of the innings Garner came in to swish his bat merrily and we finished with a total of 269.

This was a stiff target for Northamptonshire to chase, particularly after Garner had removed Larkins and Williams in his opening spell. Geoff Cook and Allan Lamb counter-attacked, adding 113 in just 13 overs, whereupon a fine throw from Peter Roebuck accounted for Cook. Pete has run out a surprising number of batsmen in his time: when the ball is hit to Richards the batsmen never contemplate a second run, to Pete they do. Often they make it, but not always. When Lamb was brilliantly stumped by Derek Taylor, victory was almost assured. Garner returned to the attack and unerringly mopped up the tail, finishing with the astonishing figures of 6 for 29. We had won the Gillette Cup by 45 runs.

We returned to a jubilant dressing room. Roy Kerslake, after two years of pacing up and down pavilions around the country, agonising over every game, breathed a massive sigh of relief. Roy, as chairman of the cricket committee, had devoted himself to this team. No problem, whether cricketing or personal, was too much trouble for him; no one had worked harder on behalf of Somerset CCC. He had acquired the respect and trust of every member of the side. We were thrilled for him, for our supporters and, of course, for ourselves.

Brian Rose led his side out onto the balcony and brandished the cup above his shoulders and the crowd roared. At last, after 104 years, Somerset had a trophy to take home to Taunton.

Afterwards we all made our way to Nottingham. Brian Rose and Peter Denning stopped off at the Watford Gap service station for some eggs, bacon and sausages, only to be greeted by coachloads of Somerset supporters who were astounded to find Somerset's captain and vice-captain in such mundane surroundings. Surely they should be sipping champagne in some exclusive London club? Of course they should have known that Dasher prefers beer (Butcombe if possible) to champagne, and sausages (with tomato sauce) to caviar.

Somerset v Northamptonshire, Gillette Cup Final
8th September, 1979

SOMERSET

*B. C. Rose, b Watts	41
P. W. Denning, c Sharp b Sarfraz	19
I. V. A. Richards, b Griffiths	117
P. M. Roebuck, b Willey	14
I. T. Botham, b T. M. Lamb	27
V. J. Marks, b Griffiths	9
G. I. Burgess, c Sharp b Watts	1
D. Breakwell, b T. M. Lamb	5
J. Garner, not out	24
†D. J. S. Taylor, not out	1
K. F. Jennings,	
Extras (b 5, l-b 3, n-b 3)	11
8 wickets 60 overs	**269**

Fall of wickets: 1/34, 2/95, 3/145, 4/186, 5/213, 6/214, 7/219, 8/268.

Bowling: Sarfraz 12–3–51–1; Griffiths 12–1–58–2; Watts 12–2–34–2; T. M. Lamb 12–0–70–2; Willey 12–2–45–1.

NORTHAMPTONSHIRE

G. Cook, run out	44
W. Larkins, lbw b Garner	0
R. G. Williams, hit wkt b Garner	8
A. J. Lamb, st Taylor b Richards	78
P. Willey, c Taylor b Garner	5
T. J. Yardley, c Richards b Burgess	20
†G. Sharp, b Garner	22
Sarfraz Nawaz, not out	16
T. M. Lamb, b Garner	4
B. J. Griffiths, b Garner	0
*P. J. Watts, absent hurt	0
Extras (b 6, l-b 9, w 5, n-b 7)	27
56.3 overs	**224**

Fall of wickets: 1/3, 2/13, 3/126, 4/138, 5/170, 6/182, 7/218, 8/224, 9/224.

Bowling: Garner 10.3–3–29–6; Botham 10–3–27–0; Jennings 12–1–29–0; Burgess 9–1–37–1; Marks 4–0–22–0; Richards 9–0–44–1; Breakwell 2–0–9–0.

Somerset won by 45 runs

Once we'd all arrived at the hotel we did our best to celebrate, but proceedings were surprisingly muted. many of us felt too drained after the final to raise the roof, so moderation, for the most part, prevailed. Anyway we had another important game the following day.

Inevitably the atmosphere in the dressing room on Sunday was far more relaxed than the previous day. Again we lost the toss and batted first. Thanks to a sterling half century by Peter Roebuck and some steady contributions from the middle order, we reached a respectable total of 185. As we entered the field after tea we knew that Middlesex were defending 182 at Canterbury. Nottinghamshire only threatened our score when Clive Rice was at the wicket. Colin Dredge produced one of his nip-backers and trapped him leg-before. Whilst we were fielding we could hear sudden bursts of applause for no apparent reason. Somerset supporters, equipped with transistor radios, were celebrating the fall of a Kent wicket. Gradually these roars became more frequent; Kent were collapsing as quickly as Nottinghamshire. When Botham captured the last wicket, news filtered through that Kent were in a hopeless position. By the time we reached the dressing room they had lost. So Rose strode onto the outfield to loft another trophy into the air.

Back inside the pavilion the champagne corks started popping again. Graham Burgess withdrew from the hubbub for a while, tied his faithful boots together, strode out on to the balcony and hung them ceremoniously on a flower basket, his career complete.

At Trent Bridge with the John Player League title. Botham, as usual, has the bottle of champagne. (Somerset County Gazette).

'Double' celebrations prompt Denning to wear a tie. Kitchen, Gard and Roebuck look on in amazement. (Somerset County Gazette).

(Below left) A well-earned drink after Dasher's brilliant 90 against Middlesex in the semi-final. (Somerset County Gazette).

(Below) Pete Denning settling down to his favourite meal. (Somerset County Gazette).

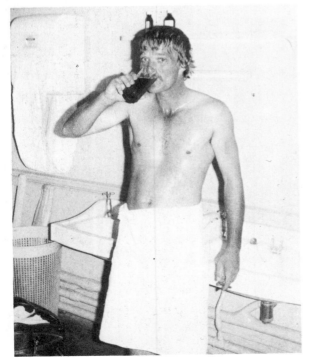

Keith Jennings, Milverton's medium pacer. (Somerset County Gazette).

Somerset v Nottinghamshire, John Player League
9th September, 1979

SOMERSET

*B. C. Rose, b Watson		4
P. W. Denning, b Rice		21
I. V. A. Richards, b Hemmings		25
P. M. Roebuck, c Birch b Watson		50
I. T. Botham, c Birch b Hemmings		30
G. I. Burgess, b Bore		6
V. J. Marks, c Randall b Cooper		14
J. Garner, c and b Rice		0
D. Breakwell, not out		8
C. H. Dredge, not out		2
†D. J. S. Taylor,		
Extras (b 8, l-b 15, n-b 2)		25

8 wickets 39 overs 185

Fall of wickets: 1/10, 2/56, 3/58, 4/114, 5/131, 6/166, 7/168, 8/182.

Bowling: Watson 8–0–27–2; Bore 8–2–18–1; Hemmings 8–0–43–2; Cooper 7–0–55–1; Rice 7–2–13–2; Tunnicliffe 1–0–4–0.

NOTTINGHAMSHIRE

S. B. Hassan, c Taylor b Botham		6
R. T. Robinson, run out		35
D. W. Randall, c Taylor b Garner		1
*C. E. B. Rice, lbw b Dredge		39
J. D. Birch, lbw b Dredge		2
H. T. Tunnicliffe, c Taylor b Burgess		5
†M. J. Harris, not out		17
E. E. Hemmings, b Richards		0
W. K. Watson, c Taylor b Garner		5
K. Cooper, b Garner		0
M. K. Bore, lbw b Botham		7
Extras (l-b 5, w 3, n-b 4)		12

33.1 overs 129

Fall of wickets: 1/11, 2/15, 3/83, 4/91, 5/91, 6/99, 7/102, 8/119, 9/119.

Bowling: Garner 6–2–16–3; Botham 5.1–0–18–2; Dredge 8–0–28–2; Burgess 7–0–40–1; Richards 7–1–15–1.

Somerset won by 56 runs

8. 1980

After two such tumultuous years the 1980 season was viewed with some trepidation: it was bound to be a difficult year. Viv Richards and Joel Garner would be touring with the West Indies, Ian Botham, newly appointed England Captain, would miss more than half of the games, and it transpired that Brian Rose would only play in twelve Championship games because of Test calls and injury.

To combat the absence of so many key players, the Somerset Committee decided to recruit Sunil Gavaskar, India's Test Captain. He joined us on the eve of a Benson & Hedges match at Canterbury; none of us, apart from Ian, knew what to expect and we were a little shy of welcoming such an established Test cricketer into our ranks. We had all marvelled at his brilliant double century against England at the Oval the previous year. That had been an innings to undermine one's patriotism, for such a performance clearly deserved to be crowned by victory. As we all gradually congregated at the bar we exchanged greetings with this polite, retiring little man, who was obviously devoid of all the trappings we have come to expect of Test stars. We retired to our bedrooms after a long drive from Birmingham and wondered whether Sunil could adapt immediately to the special demands of one-day cricket.

The next day we discovered that he most certainly could. Requiring 243 to win, Rose and Gavaskar added 241 in just 43 overs. Rose played superbly, ending his innings in swashbuckling style by hitting off-spinner Charlie Rowe for six sixes in the space of two overs. The balcony, however, was more interested in Gavaskar. Our first observation, apart from the legendary straightness of his bat, was his ability to judge a single to perfection. Sunil, on his own admission, is not a brilliant sprinter, but in the opening overs singles were stolen without any trace of misunderstanding: it could have been Rose and Denning.

His footwork and timing were quite astonishing. Twice he tiptoed down the wicket to Underwood, still found himself short of the ball and yet followed through on the up to drive him past mid off with remarkable power. A deft flick of the wrists and the ball disappeared over the ropes at square leg – not just a few yards over but into Botham country ten rows back. Occasionally, after a rare rash stroke, we saw him cup his face like a horse wearing blinkers and stare down the wicket in order to regain concentration. Comparisons with Richards were fruitless but inevitable.

The following week he scored an equally brilliant 123 against Middlesex's international attack (Daniel, Van der Bilj, Selvey, Emburey and Edmonds), although we lost by one run in another nerve-racking one-day finish. Brian Rose was prompted to remark, 'Sometimes I find myself just standing there and watching down the wicket. I have never seen such technical brilliance'[16].

Sunil quickly settled into the Somerset dressing room. No one who is unable to locate the hand brake on his car can remain aloof for long. Botham nicknamed him 'Swoop' because of his ponderous movements in the field and his absolute refusal to dive under any circumstances. Peter Roebuck observed:

> Where most fieldsmen hurry towards the ball to intercept it more easily, Swoop ambles along leaving it until the last possible minute to dart out a hand and effect the stop. Naturally this produces tremendous applause from the crowd accompanied by an outrageously innocent smile from Gavaskar.[4]

We quickly began to appreciate his mischievous sense of humour which often surfaced in the form of understatement. After we had endured a terrible pounding from the Derbyshire batsmen, he quietly observed that 'our bowlers seem a little more friendly than theirs.' Quite often they were, in 1980.

When we all gathered in a bar in Northampton to bid him farewell, any shyness had long since disappeared and we enjoyed chatting to him as he indulged in a rare alcoholic spree. Indeed, everyone had been delighted to have the Gavaskars in Taunton, not only Sunil but his wife Marshniel and precocious son Rohan who hero-worships Viv Richards. I think that he enjoyed his brief foray into county cricket as well. Back in Bombay he's unable to take his family to the shops for fear of being mobbed by admirers, but he felt utterly secure visiting the County Stores in Taunton. He left us wondering where this unassuming, gentle man hid that core of toughness which has

John Player League v Notts 1980. The Marks cover drive to
third man – as usual. (Somerset County Gazette).

Pete Roebuck plays my favourite shot. (Somerset County Gazette).

An action photo of Colin Dredge. Close to the stumps, left leg straight and his eyes are open! (Somerset County Gazette).

Six Somerset representatives at Headingley, 1980 – England v West Indies. (Somerset County Gazette).

(Below) Watching Gavaskar and Rose at Kent. As the partnership developed, Roy Kerslake, Chairman of the Cricket Committee, was not allowed to remove the hat. (Somerset County Gazette).

enabled him to dominate bowlers around the world for the last decade.

In the absence of Rose and Botham I captained the side on several occasions in 1980. I found the Championship matches less demanding than the John Player League games. There was time to consult and come to a decision about the right bowlers and field placings for a particular batsman. I'd take the opportunity to stand at first slip alongside Derek Taylor, Peter Roebuck and Sunil, and between us some sort of plan of attack would emerge. In the John Player League it was different. Decisions had to be made on the spur of the moment and my advisers were spreadeagled all round the ground. Should Hallam bowl his eight overs at once or must we save him to the end? Should square leg save the single or the boundary? Why is my best boundary fielder at short mid wicket? Have I distributed the overs correctly or will we be stranded with Peter Denning defending six runs off the last over? Why didn't I pick an extra bowler anyway? Where does this batsman like to hit the ball? Does he prefer facing seamers or spinners? Why hasn't Popplewell bowled that maiden over I demanded? It's no wonder that Brian Rose begins to look a little jaded by the end of August.

My brief spell as captain certainly helped me to appreciate the value of men such as Hallam Moseley and Colin Dredge. In a weakened bowling side both were prepared to bowl all day if necessary. In September Colin was deservedly voted 'Player of the Season', being easily our leading wicket taker.

Colin was spotted by Somerset as a club cricketer for Frome: most Frome sides of the seventies contained at least five Dredges, so I can only presume that we signed the correct one. At first glance he still bowls like a club cricketer. Off a short run he slings the ball down with an ungainly catapult action. The whole process is neither fluid nor rhythmic, but he still manages to obey the basic principles of getting close to the stumps and keeping his arm high. Throughout his career he has developed the happy knack of dismissing more than his fair share of world class players. His first wicket in county cricket was Glen Turner, and Zaheer Abbas has good reason to treat the 'Demon of Frome' with special respect.

His most dangerous ball is his 'nip-backer', the one

The county ground in 1980. Notice the proximity of the churchyard and the River Tone, also the skeleton of the new pavilion. (Somerset County Gazette).

Sunil awarded his county cap by Ian Botham. (Somerset County Gazette).

that shoots into the right hander's pads like a fast off break. Recently he has developed an outrageous slower ball: I've yet to see him take a wicket with it but he assures me that it 'keeps 'em guessing.' Occasionally, almost apologetically, he'll bowl a bouncer.

Over the last six years Colin has been a crucial cog in Somerset's one-day bowling machine. Invariably he's been asked to bowl when the batsmen are slogging, without the opportunity to deliver a few cheap overs when they are playing properly. Sometimes his analyses have suffered as a result, but Colin has never complained. If there's a gale blowing you can be sure that Colin will be bowling into it. It's not

surprising that his team mates hold him in such high regard.

His batting has changed over the years. In the good old days it was a simple operation for 'Bert'. He would plunge his right leg as far down the wicket as possible and then start trying to locate the ball. We used to cringe when he went merrily through this procedure even when facing Colin Croft and Malcolm Marshall. However it proved most effective. Unfortunately he's become more worldly wise now: proper batsmen play the fast men off the back foot so he has decided to do the same. Admittedly this has reduced his likelihood of being hit on the head and I think that his wife and family have welcomed the change in technique, but it doesn't seem to produce as many runs. However he still manages to play at least one memorable innings

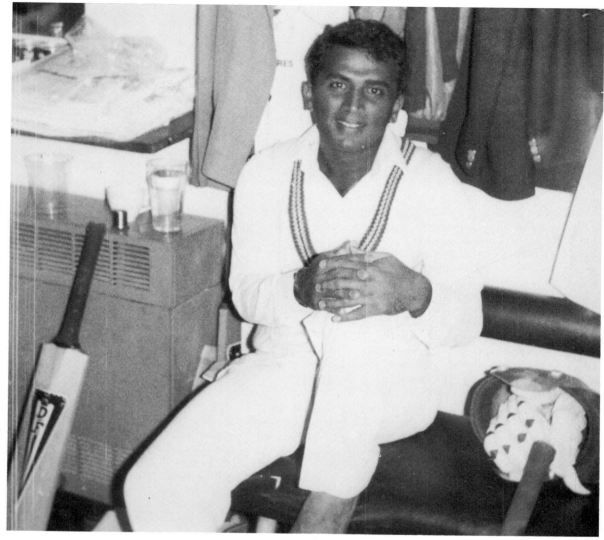

Sunil Gavaskar quickly settled into the Somerset dressing room. (Somerset County Gazette).

each year. In 1983 he had the impudence to reach his 50 by backhand sweeping Underwood for 4 and then swotting him over mid wicket for 6. Men of Frome are not impressed by reputation alone.

In the winter he plays centre forward for Frome Town. We were all amazed to hear that he has been sent off the field twice in his career because 'he kicked me so I thumped him'. He's certainly made no enemies on the cricket field where he embodies all the traditional values of county cricket.

Somehow we contrived to finish fourth in the Championship, despite winning only three games. Northamptonshire, who won five, finished twelfth,

but let the justice of that be debated elsewhere. It was back to normal in the John Player League as we ended the season runners up. In the last game of the season we defeated the Champions, Warwickshire, by 26 runs, but by then it was too late. In Somerset's innings Derek Taylor was out obstructing the field. Finding himself stranded in the middle of the wicket he kicked the ball from under Willis's hands and immediately set off for the pavilion. Everyone was highly amused by this uncharacteristically flamboyant gesture from Derek. Hours later he still could not explain why he did it; at least it was reassuring to know that even the most sensible of men are prone to the occasional aberration of the brain.

9. 1981

At the start of the 1981 season we drove past the Jack White gates to enter the ground at the new Priory Bridge entrance. The old brown scoreboard – 'Colditz' – had been demolished and in its place was a massive red brick pavilion – a symbol of the change in Somerset's fortunes over the last decade.

The new building, which was officially opened by Peter May on 25th May, has met with almost universal approval. It contains two spacious dressing rooms, three bars, a well-equipped kitchen, a function room which can accommodate anything from discos to chess tournaments, and offices for the administrative staff.

Visiting teams in particular have welcomed the pavilion. In the past we reckoned that the dungeon, which served as the away dressing room in the old pavilion, was worth at least 50 runs a game. Opposition batsmen had to crane their necks to follow the action. Fast bowlers flexing their shoulder muscles were liable to suffer severe dislocations to their bowling arm. Twelfth men were driven to drink in an effort to procure hot water for their elders: unless they turned on the taps at 3.30, all the hot water available would end up in the home dressing room. Nor had the old kitchens allowed much variety for visiting gourmands – either chicken salad or ham salad. Now Mrs Webb, our catering manager, is beloved by all visiting county cricketers. They all look forward to coming to Taunton (especially if Garner is resting); there is hot water, there are sumptuous meals and room to essay a practice cover drive in the dressing room – I think we're spoiling them.

The new pavilion also possesses a physio room, and within a month we had a physiotherapist to occupy it. Dennis Waight came to Somerset from Sydney via the West Indian cricket team. When Kerry Packer established World Series cricket he insisted that every side should be properly attended to and he employed Dennis to look after the West Indians. Clive Lloyd and company were so impressed by his work that they have kept him ever since.

Dennis looks like an ex-boxer, which is hardly surprising, because he is. He has also swum and played rugby league to a high level in Australia; strangely cricket was never one of his sports. All of our players – and several of us are not known for the attention we pay to our physical condition – value the impact that Dennis has made.

His aim is to keep everyone fit and available for selection for every game. Just as politicians (one hopes) aim for zero unemployment, his goal is inevitably unattainable, but the fact that Clive Lloyd, who possesses the knees of an octogenarian, is still playing is a tribute to his skill.

Before each game we will spend 10–15 minutes with Dennis, who will supervise a variety of bizarre stretching exercises of his own invention. If the weather is dry, early arrivals at the county ground are greeted by the sight of a dozen tracksuits spreadeagled on the grass with arms and legs sticking out all over the place. It must look ridiculous and I've often wondered how Jack White or Bill Andrews would have reacted to the whole procedure. But it seems to work and none of us have had the courage to tell Dennis what he can do with his exercises. For he is a tough man. Most days he'll complete a nine-mile run just to keep himself in shape and to work up a thirst for the evening. He doesn't pretend to possess any cricketing expertise and has never been known to criticise a player's performance on the field. But if you're not stretching your hamstrings sufficiently he'll readily draw upon his own mysterious Australian vocabulary to produce greater efforts.

As well as tuning up the body for the rigours of the coming day, I think the fact that we all gather and go through a set routine each day helps to prepare us mentally. For there are occasional damp Thursdays in Northampton when not everyone is cockahoop about the prospect of playing cricket.

During a game he has a stabilizing effect on us all; he remains phlegmatic and approachable whatever the circumstances. In the evenings he can be relied upon to frequent the hotel bar at least until Sergeant Bilko comes to our screens. Last year he stunned us all by declaring that he was going to change this routine. 'What's he up to?' we all wondered. 'Is he going to the cinema or the theatre or to read a book?' Eventually he announced, 'Tonight I'm going out . . . to the pub.'

On 22nd July we played our first game in the Nat West Trophy and lost comfortably at Northampton. At least we had the compensation of knowing that we

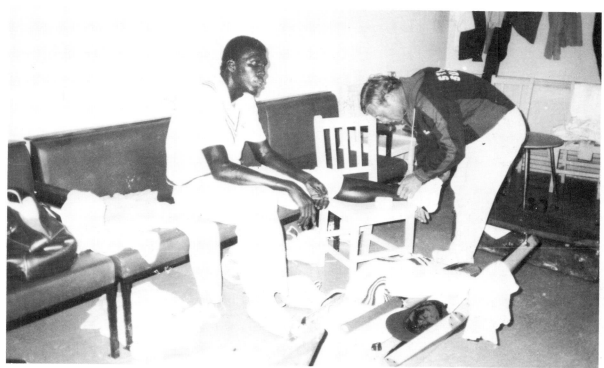

Dennis Waight tends Joel Garner. (Somerset County Gazette).

Dennis Waight at work with Somerset's opening bowlers. (Somerset County Gazette).

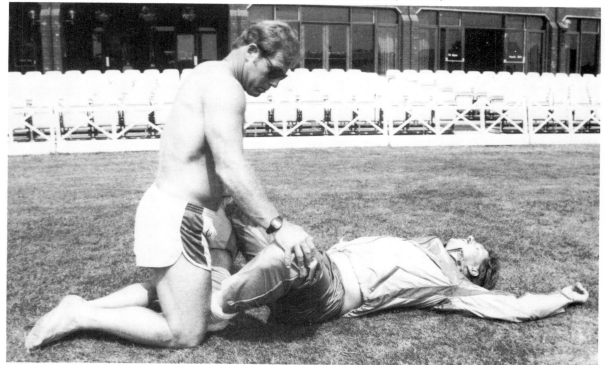

Who's won the Man of the Match Award? Benson & Hedges quarter final v Kent 1981. (Somerset County Gazette).

Nigel Popplewell. Tom Graveney is the adjudicator. (Somerset County Gazette).

Mid wicket conference with Joel: 'no quick singles'. (Somerset County Gazette).

would be making one appearance in a Lord's final on the following Saturday, against Surrey in the Benson & Hedges final.

In the semi-final Kent had been defeated by five wickets at Taunton. No doubt remembering their wretched experiences of 1979, they batted limply against a keen Somerset attack. After early setbacks the Cantabs, Roebuck and Popplewell, added 67 when the match was in the balance.

Surrey had lost their two previous Lord's finals in 1979 and 1980 and the strained faces of their early batsmen betrayed the tension in the Surrey camp. Jack Richards, their makeshift opener, was quickly bowled by Garner. They did not reach double figures until the thirteenth over, whereupon the Somerset crowd burst into a round of ironic applause. Even

though we were playing against Surrey in London, our supporters appeared to outnumber theirs by five to one. This has been the feature of all Somerset's finals: our crowd are determined to make their presence felt; as a result the opposition sense that they are playing in hostile, rather than neutral, territory.

Only Roger Knight, Surrey's captain, with a brave 92, seemed equal to the occasion and he guided the Surrey total to 194 for 8. In reply Somerset lost Rose and Denning for 5 leaving Richards and Roebuck to repair the damage. They added 105. Although Pete Roebuck only scored 22 of these runs his contribution was vital as he weathered an extremely hostile spell from Sylvester Clarke, one of the most feared bowlers in the game. Botham replaced Roebuck and within 13 overs the match was over. Richards reached his century off 111 deliveries, whereupon both players began to enjoy themselves, despatching the Surrey bowlers to the boundary at will. The match and a

Somerset v Surrey, Benson & Hedges Cup Final
25th July, 1981

SURREY

G. S. Clinton, c Roebuck b Marks	6
†C. J. Richards, b Garner	1
*R. D. V. Knight, c Taylor b Garner	92
G. P. Howarth, c Roebuck b Marks	16
M. A. Lynch, c Garner b Popplewell	22
D. M. Smith, b Garner	7
S. T. Clarke, c Popplewell b Garner	15
G. R. T. Roope, not out	14
D. J. Thomas, b Garner	0
R. D. Jackman, not out	2
P. I. Pocock,	
Extras (b 2, l-b 14, w 2, n-b 1)	19

8 wickets   55 overs   194

Fall of wickets: 1/4, 2/16, 3/63, 4/98, 5/132, 6/166, 7/182, 8/183.

Bowling: Garner 11–5–14–5; Botham 11–2–44–0; Dredge 11–0–48–0; Marks 11–5–24–2; Popplewell 11–0–45–1.

SOMERSET

*B. C. Rose, b Jackman	5
P. W. Denning, b Clarke	0
I. V. A. Richards, not out	132
P. M. Roebuck, c Smith b Knight	22
I. T. Botham, not out	37
N. F. M. Popplewell,	
V. J. Marks,	
D. Breakwell,	
J. Garner,	
†D. J. S. Taylor,	
C. H. Dredge,	
Extras (n-b 1)	1

3 wickets   44.3 overs   197

Fall of wickets: 1/5, 2/5, 3/110.

Bowling: Clarke 8–1–24–1; Jackman 11–1–53–0; Thomas 5.3–0–32–0; Pocock 11–1–46–0; Knight 9–0–41–1.

Somerset won by 7 wickets

---

these three occasions were 5–38, 6–29 and 5–14. Joel was by now recognised as the most effective one-day bowler in the world and obviously not overawed by the big occasion. At the start of an innings he will attack with three slips, a gully and a short leg. Sensible batsmen are content with survival. His ability to obtain steep bounce from a good length will keep the waiting slip cordon on tenterhooks. Occasionally he'll spear in his deadly yorker. At the end of a one-day game he is a superb container. He usually aims to bowl a succession of straight yorkers which are impossible to slog. Should the batsman have the temerity to advance down the wicket, he runs the risk of facing the ultimate deterrent, his bouncer.

His height and control, as well as his speed, ensure respect wherever he plays. Perhaps his only failings as a fast bowler are that he's too intelligent and goodnatured. Certainly he doesn't enjoy hitting opposition batsmen. He realises, too, that fast bowlers need to pace themselves throughout a season and a career. So on occasions he'll rely upon his ability to cut the ball off the wicket rather than on sheer pace.

However, when motivated, he can be a horrifying prospect. Lancashire batsmen know this to their cost, for in 1978, during his spell with Littleborough in the Lancashire League, the county side rejected him. Joel does not forget easily. Those who have survived one of his raucous appeals for caught behind have learnt to sway onto the back foot thereafter.

Joel at Lord's v Surrey. Viv is Man of the Match again! (Somerset County Gazette).

---

new trophy for the cupboard was won with ten overs to spare. Viv Richards was named Man of the Match, having completed a hat trick of centuries in Lord's finals – 138* in the World Cup against England, 117 v Northamptonshire in 1979 and 132* v Surrey, each time winning the award.

Spare a thought for Joel Garner whose figures on

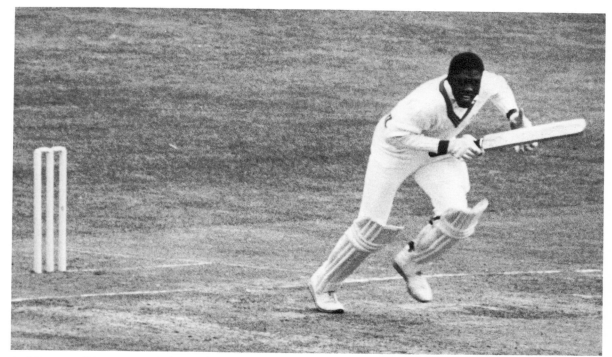

Joel Garner – off he goes on another suicidal run. (Somerset County Gazette).

Off the field he possesses the best toothy grin in the game. Often he will choose to amble around the ground during a match and indulge in some conversation with the locals. Whether these conversations ever lead anywhere I doubt, as after five years we still have difficulty deciphering what he's talking about in the dressing room. If Viv, Joel and Hallam are locked in debate we don't even bother to listen. Children especially warm to him, perhaps because he never disappoints the hordes of autograph hunters, or perhaps they can detect more quickly the generous nature of his personality.

His batting is well worth watching. It is characterised by powerful lofted straight drives and appalling running between the wickets. At the beginning of the 1983 season he informed us that he had 'done swiping', by which he meant that he had given up trying to smash every ball out of the ground and that he would concentrate on playing properly. There has been no discernible change.

Inevitably we finished second in the John Player League in 1981, Essex winning the trophy by a comfortable margin. The most memorable match was against Hampshire on 23rd August, for it was one of those rare occasions when Botham and Richards went berserk at the same time. It's impossible to describe the mayhem that they inflicted on the Hampshire attack, so I'll merely furnish you with the statistics and let your imagination wander.

Ian Botham scored 106 in 67 minutes off 72 balls. His first 50 came in 52 minutes from 54 balls, with two sixes and four fours. His second 50 came in nine minutes from 13 balls, with five sixes and four fours. Altogether there were 39 scoring strokes. With Viv Richards he added 179 runs in 67 minutes from 21 overs, a John Player League fifth wicket record. They added 100 in 50 minutes from 16.2 overs. The next fifty came in six minutes from 18 balls. Altogether the partnership lasted for 128 balls, Richards scoring 66 from 56 balls. At one stage 76 runs were recorded in four overs, Botham scoring 58 (48–106) and Richards 17 (65–82) with one wide.

By the way, we managed to win that game.

In the Championship, after a sluggish start, we enjoyed one of our best seasons, recording seven victories from our last nine games and finishing behind Nottinghamshire and Sussex.

Our recent Championship performances have been frustrating for players and supporters alike. A pattern has developed over the years. We tend to begin the season with a series of drawn matches, relying upon a sprint at the end to reach respectability. If only we

Two backroom boys, Jock McCombe and Dennis Waight, enjoying the comforts of the new pavilion. (Somerset County Gazette).

Nigel Popplewell with the Benson & Hedges Cup. (Somerset County Gazette).

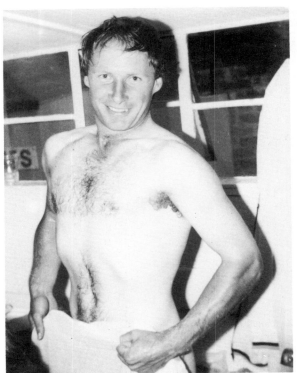

It's me. The problem that confronts Dennis Waight each year. (Somerset County Gazette).

Rose hoists the Benson & Hedges trophy after victory against Surrey. (Somerset County Gazette).

We amuse early arrivals at Taunton with some of Dennis' exercises.

Richards and Botham went berserk against Hampshire – John Player League at Taunton, August 23rd, 1981.

Benson & Hedges Final v Surrey 1981. Brian Rose shows the Benson & Hedges trophy to the fans. (Somerset County Gazette).

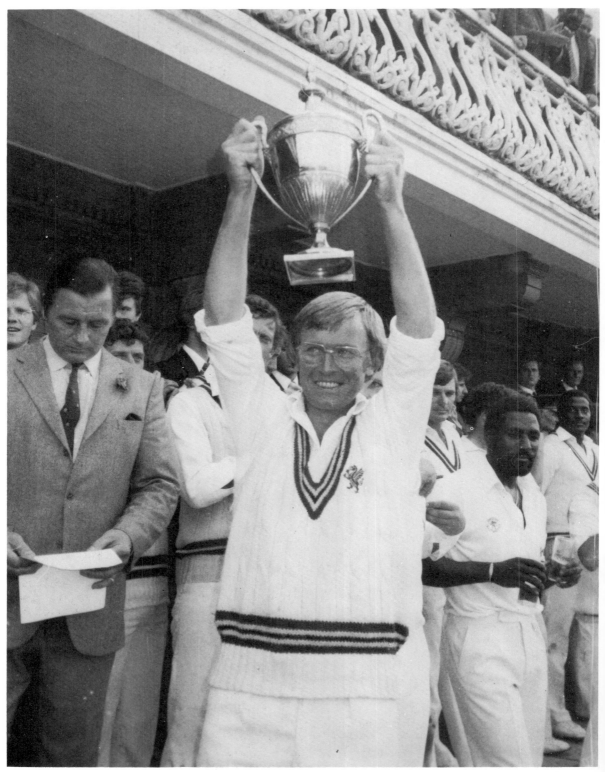

Brian Rose with the Benson & Hedges trophy. (Somerset County Gazette).

Peter May opens the new pavilion on 25 May 1981. Colin Atkinson, Chairman Geoff Lawson and Terry Alderman look on. (Somerset County Gazette).

could reach the end of July in the top five we would have an excellent chance of winning the most coveted of the domestic competitions. For by August some sides begin to wilt, they lose their early-season doggedness and the likes of Garner and Richards are more likely to dominate them.

Our own attitude leaves room for improvement. Our continual involvement in the more glamorous one-day competitions has resulted in us relaxing too much in the hard grind of Championship cricket. This is the one major hurdle that the present Somerset side has yet to overcome. We have not shown the stamina and perseverance necessary to maintain the highest standards day in, day out. This should remain our highest priority in the future. A really professional team does not require 10,000 spectators or TV cameras to perform to its potential.

However, in 1981 we sensed the possibility of Championship success. The surge began at Sheffield at the beginning of August, when we recorded our first victory on Yorkshire soil since 1902. As usual there were grave mutterings around the ground as Colin Dredge (6–43) swept past any second innings resistance.

By the time we reached Folkestone on 26th August, we felt that we could snatch the Championship if the two leaders slipped up. Against Kent we produced one of our best Championship performances. On a pitch that suited Underwood as the glass slipper fitted Cinderella we were unfortunate to lose the toss, thereby forfeiting the chance of batting when the wicket was at its best. Nonetheless Kent were dismissed for 186. On the first evening Underwood was introduced after five overs and was soon making the ball turn and lift sharply.

After an early flourish, Jerry Lloyds was replaced by Richards. Viv always relishes the challenge of facing Underwood and the duel is a tremendous

The big bird in full flight.

a fascinating, if slow, day's cricket as Somerset's batsmen adopted different methods to combat the threat of the Kent spinners. Rose used his pad as a second (and often first) line of defence and relied upon deflections on the leg side; Roebuck, watchful as a hawk, kept withdrawing his bat at the last possible moment; Denning somehow contrived to tickle Underwood past first slip for the majority of his runs. Underwood eventually took seven wickets, but it took him 54 overs.

The Kent side realised that they had missed their chance and, despite Asif's determination, quickly succumbed in the second innings. As soon as we left the field several members of our side turned to the cricket scores to find out about our rivals' progress. To our dismay they had also won. Let's hope we can muster the same urgency in the years to come.

Championship Table, 1981 – Bonus Points

	P	W	L	D	Bt	Bl	Pts
Nottinghamshire	21	11	4	6	56	72	304
Sussex	20	11	3	6	58	68	302
Somerset	22	10	2	10	54	65	279
Middlesex	21	9	3	9	49	64	257

Joel keeps smiling despite the English weather. (Somerset County Gazette).

spectacle as two great craftsmen probe each other's weaknesses. Viv counter-attacked brilliantly, driving 'Deadly' through mid wicket as if the pitch were flawless. Underwood was beginning to wear his harassed look when, to his relief, he bowled Viv just before stumps. On his return to the pavilion Viv was furious with himself: he had been looking forward to renewing the contest in the morning and stretching his ability to the limit.

The next day we had little expectation of passing Kent's total, but Rose (three and a half hours), Roebuck (four hours) and Denning, whose innings of 98 was surely one of his best for Somerset, somehow survived long enough to ensure a lead of 123. It was

Ian Botham lashes out against Surrey in the Benson & Hedges
Final, 1981. (Wyvern Sports Marketing Ltd).

Somerset supporters make their presence felt in the tavern at
Lord's. (Somerset County Gazette).

Somerset v Kent at Folkestone

26th, 27th and 28th August, 1981

KENT

First Innings			Second Innings	
R. A. Woolmer, c Garner b Dredge		11	lbw b Garner	0
M. R. Benson, c Taylor b Marks		11	c Taylor b Marks	0
N. Taylor, b Garner		3	c Richards b Garner	0
*Asif Iqbal, c and b Dredge		2	c Rose b Marks	45
C. S. Cowdrey, c Garner b Marks		7	c Taylor b Marks	25
G. W. Johnson, b Garner		27	lbw b Dredge	3
R. M. Ellison, not out		61	c Dredge b Marks	9
E. A. Baptiste, c Rose b Marks		33	b Marks	15
†S. N. Waterton, c Taylor b Moseley		10	b Garner	4
D. L. Underwood, c Rose b Moseley		7	b Garner	1
K. B. Jarvis, b Garner		0	not out	1
Extras (b 2, l-b 3, n-b 8)		13	Extras (b 6, l-b 4, n-b 8)	18
		186		121

Fall of wickets: 1/26, 2/26, 3/31, 4/38, 5/38, 6/93, 7/133, 8/158, 9/171.

1/4, 2/4, 3/8, 4/57, 5/76, 6/88, 7/100, 8/107, 9/114.

Bowling: *First Innings*: Garner 19.2–4–53–3; Moseley 13–4–28–2; Marks 25–12–48–3; Dredge 15–6–33–2; Lloyds 1–0–4–0; Richards 4–1–7–0.

Second Innings: Garner 19–8–37–4; Dredge 6–3–20–1; Marks 29.3–14–34–5; Richards 1–0–1–0; Lloyds 8–4–11–0.

SOMERSET

First Innings

*B. C. Rose, st Waterton b Johnson		39
J. W. Lloyds, b Underwood		25
I. V. A. Richards, b Underwood		37
P. M. Roebuck, c Taylor b Underwood		51
P. W. Denning, c Jarvis b Underwood		98
N. F. M. Popplewell, c Taylor b Johnson		21
V. J. Marks, b Johnson		0
†D. J. S. Taylor, c Asif b Underwood		4
J. Garner, lbw b Underwood		0
H. R. Moseley, c Taylor b Underwood		3
C. H. Dredge, not out		4
Extras (b 3, l-b 9, n-b 15)		27
		309

Fall of wickets: 1/35, 2/83, 3/119, 4/215, 5/250, 6/254, 7/270, 8/270, 9/278.

Bowling: Jarvis 13–2–41–0; Baptiste 6–1–12–0; Johnson 54–19–107–3; Underwood 54.4–19–118–7; Ellison 1–0–4–0.

Somerset won by an innings and 2 runs

10. 1982

Our defence of the Benson & Hedges Cup began shakily in 1982. Having been humiliated by Middlesex at Lord's we scrambled through to the quarter finals after victories against the Combined Universities, Glamorgan and Gloucestershire.

The match against the Combined Universities produced a remarkable world record and the Man of the Match award for Derek Taylor. He took eight catches during the Universities innings of 147. None were spectacular but all effortlessly taken – the hallmark of Derek's wicketkeeping.

Derek had learnt his trade at Surrey under the wing of Arthur McIntyre. A regular first team spot was blocked by Arnold Long, so in 1970 he moved to the West Country and never regretted his decision. Like all good wicketkeepers his contributions were rarely noticed – only their catastrophic blunders make the headlines. Derek made very few. Standing up to Tom Cartwright and Graham Burgess he looked international class : miraculous leg-side stumpings were commonplace. In fact he played for the MCC and in a Test trial but was never able to oust the more obvious talents of Alan Knott and Bob Taylor.

For two seasons (1974–75) he opened the batting successfully – a tribute to his stamina. After five and a half hours in the field his wicketkeeping pads would quickly be replaced by sturdier batting ones and he'd stroll out to survive that dreaded half hour at the end of the day. He batted within his limitations, specialising in square drives on the off side and deflections to leg. Occasionally his slow scoring frustrated our more impatient supporters but the cries of 'C'mon Taylor', were quietly ignored as he set about building his innings at his own pace.

As Close's vice-captain he was invaluable, often papering over the administrative cracks of his leader. Close himself appreciated Derek's efforts : 'He was the most responsible player in the side, quietly thinking about his game and turning out good performances behind the wicket day after day, season after season.'[9]

Deputising for Close, he was a methodical and cautious captain, which is hardly surprising having been brought up in the old school of Surrey CCC. After Close's departure his experience provided an important ballast in the youthful sides of 1978/9.

Once Graham Burgess had retired he was the only survivor of the sixties. Occasionally he must have felt exasperated by the impetuous youths around him, no doubt contemplating the change in attitude of young professionals during his twenty years in the game. However, he easily adapted to the changing face of cricket, despite his insistence on wearing long johns until the end of May and his leisurely running between the wickets. He always remained eager to help youngsters on the staff and Trevor Gard in particular appreciates the attention he received during his long apprenticeship in the second team.

Derek enjoyed being part of the county cricket scene right until his retirement. After the game he would seek out his diminishing band of contemporaries and swop anecdotes and gossip over gins and tonics. He is now successfully established in Sydney but I bet that each April his fingers start twitching and he wonders what his old sparring partners are up to.

Our passage to the final was relatively straightforward. Kent were beaten – yet again – at Canterbury, Derek squeezing the winning runs from the final over. In the semi-final Sussex were demolished by eight wickets in front of a capacity Taunton crowd, so on 23rd July we travelled up to Lord's to face Nottinghamshire.

Before each final we have our only team dinner of the year. I'm never sure how productive they are. Everyone sits down and enjoys an excellent meal and several glasses of wine. Over the cheese and biscuits the gathering is called to order and we resolve to discuss our opponents. Everyone is invited to contribute and most do, usually at the same time. By this stage of the evening our opponents are either capable of defeating the 1948 Australians or unable to overcome Stogumber Second XI, depending on who is talking.

On this occasion Pete Roebuck, who had never faced Hadlee, was informed that he was quicker than Joel but moved the ball both ways, information hardly conducive to a sound night's sleep for Somerset's opener. Ian Botham decided that we should keep the ball up to Hadlee when he batted and the following day greeted him with a succession of bouncers – maybe he suspected a mole in our ranks.

Otherwise the remarks are the same no matter whom we are playing. Derek brands most of the

Floodlight cricket comes to Taunton. West Indies v Somerset – a benefit match for Viv. 6,000 watched the first floodlit match on an English county ground. (Somerset County Gazette).

opposition as cheats, since his encyclopaedic memory recalls at least one occasion when they failed to walk for a catch behind. Dasher shuns any technical discussion and demands that we fight. 'Both' declares that we are better than them. Viv and Joel want us to guard against complacency. Nigel Popplewell delivers brief analyses of opposition batsmen, whether he's played against them or not: 'Robinson – on side player. Birch off side – hits ball in air.'

We're quite likely to spend twenty minutes discussing Hendrick's batting and Randall's bowling. Brian Rose, having made a few opening remarks, sits back in his chair with a cigar and quietly waits for proceedings to come to an end. Eventually we all decide to let the opposition do the worrying, finish off the claret and slip happily up to our rooms. I'm bound to say, having been successful in four out of five finals, the system has something to commend it.

The final was an anticlimax for any non-partisan supporters. The Nottingham batsmen appeared paralysed by the occasion. Garner produced his deadly yorker early on; Randall and Rice both got into a tangle against my off spinners. Hallam Moseley, appearing in his first final, bowled a nervous first over conceding eleven runs, and thereafter bowled 10 overs for just 15. Garner returned to dismiss Hadlee and with Botham prevented their tail from wagging so that we needed just 131 to win.

Maybe Viv was slightly disappointed that he had no chance to amass another Lord's century. Instead he had to settle for an undefeated 50 as he and Peter Roebuck took us serenely to victory with 22 overs to spare. The loudest cheers at the presentation ceremony were for Hallam who had waited so patiently for his winner's medal. Pete Roebuck, in his new role as opening batsman, had failed only once during the entire competition and might have won the Man of the Match award at Lord's if it had not been for the remarkable perspicacity of the adjudicator, Tom Graveney, who gave it to me.

Pete has been content to be one of the unsung heroes amidst Somerset's success over the last six years. His style at the crease does not demand

Peter Roebuck – maybe he's an amateur at heart. (Somerset County Gazette).

Somerset v Nottinghamshire, Benson & Hedges Cup Final
24th July, 1982

NOTTINGHAMSHIRE		SOMERSET	
P. A. Todd, b Garner	2	P. M. Roebuck, not out	53
R. T. Robinson, c Richards b Dredge	13	P. W. Denning, c French b Hendrick	22
D. W. Randall, b Marks	19	I. V. A. Richards, not out	51
S. B. Hassan, c Taylor b Dredge	26	*B. C. Rose,	
*C. E. B. Rice, b Marks	27	I. T. Botham,	
J. D. Birch, b Moseley	7	N. F. M. Popplewell,	
R. J. Hadlee, b Garner	11	V. J. Marks,	
†B. N. French, c Taylor b Botham	8	†D. J. S. Taylor,	
E. E. Hemmings, b Botham	1	J. Garner,	
K. E. Cooper, b Garner	3	C. H. Dredge,	
M. Hendrick, not out	0	H. R. Moseley,	
Extras (l-b 5, w 7, n-b 1)	13	Extras (b 5, w 1)	6

50.1 overs 130

Fall of wickets: 1/3, 2/40, 3/40, 4/86, 5/102, 6/106, 7/122, 8/123, 9/130.

Bowling: Garner 8.1–1–13–3; Botham 9–3–19–2; Dredge 11–2–35–2; Moseley 11–2–26–1; Marks 11–4–24–2.

1 wicket 33.1 overs 132

Fall of wickets: 1/27.

Bowling: Hadlee 9–0–37–0; Hendrick 8–0–26–1; Cooper 5.1–0–41–0; Rice 6–2–11–0; Hemmings 5–0–11–0.

Somerset won by 9 wickets

Peter Roebuck, opening batsman, writer and my roommate for the last ten years.

He requires a challenge when batting: he's unlikely to score runs in a dead situation, but his mind is razor sharp when a match is to be won or saved. His intense concentration is apparent to all: TV cameras often catch him talking quietly to himself as the bowler approaches. Body and mind must be as prepared as possible to combat each delivery.

Pete is quick to assess the peculiarities of a wicket. If the bounce is steep he'll adapt by playing predominantly off the back foot, if low off the front foot. When the ball is turning sharply he has mastered a technique to prevent the ball popping into the hands of short leg by relaxing his grip on the bat and merely allowing the ball to hit it. Now, along with Richards, he is the best defensive player of spin in the club. The advent of a new bowling machine in 1983 saw him practising each morning for fifteen minutes in the indoor nets, with a specific aim in mind. He repeatedly drove balls through the off side and the improvement of his batting in the middle was obvious. Thus he uses his powers of analysis to improve his cricket as well as in furthering his reputation as a cricket writer.

Occasionally he will allow the strictures he imposes on himself to be released. In an end of season match against Northumberland in 1983, he demolished a respectable minor counties side with an inventiveness and flair that not even Richards or Botham could have surpassed. Usually in county games he shuns such methods, as we rely upon him to provide much-needed solidity to our batting. He has also become remarkably adept at the one-day game: he may not hit a succession of scintillating boundaries but he has developed a technique which ensures that he scores off an unusually high proportion of balls received.

I have roomed with Pete for ten years and we have kept each other sane (most of the time), chuckling at the absurdities of playing cricket for a living. In a small group he will lay aside his on-field image of taciturn detachment and hold forth entertainingly on any topic, ranging from the problems facing Keith Burkinshaw to those of Mrs Thatcher or Mrs Gandhi. His intellect and his preference for the occasional (?) glass of wine in a small restaurant rather than several pints in a crowded bar make him a rare breed among county cricketers. A rain-ruined Saturday in London will find him visiting two or even three theatres rather than huddling up in front of 'Grandstand'. Despite his constant criticism of my navigation, as well as my driving, we still travel together and somehow have remained good friends over the years.

We did not threaten to win any of the other

attention: there are no frills or extravagant flourishes. Even when he drives a ball to the mid-wicket boundary he remains unmoved by the sweetness of the shot, almost as if he regrets the attention that he has drawn to himself. For much of his career he has been sandwiched between Richards and Botham in the batting order, a position bringing stability to the innings but hardly thrusting him into the limelight.

Pete does not play cricket just for fun but to stretch his physical and mental resources to their limits. On leaving Cambridge with a first class honours degree in Law, he preferred cricket as a career to the possibility of being one of our leading barristers. Having made that choice, he devotes himself completely to being a successful first class cricketer lest he should regret his decision. Thus he feels the agonies of failure more acutely than most.

Celebrating the Benson & Hedges win v Kent in 1982 at Canterbury. Derek has a beer with two admirers. (Somerset County Gazette).

Denning encouraged to drink some champagne after victory against Nottingham in the Benson & Hedges Final, 1982. (Somerset County Gazette).

Hallam collects his first Lord's winners medal from Hubert Doggart. (Somerset County Gazette).

Pete Roebuck prefers a quiet drink with friends to several pints in a crowded bar. (Somerset County Gazette).

competitions that year. After two victories in the Nat West we were unceremoniously despatched from the competition by Alvin Kallicharan who played one of the finest one-day innings I can remember. Even Joel was deposited over the square leg boundary with a rapid flick of the wrists and an impish grin. We even failed to finish second in the John Player League.

However there were compensations, notably the emergence of Jerry Lloyds. In a drawn game with Northampton he achieved the feat of scoring two undefeated centuries. Throughout the match Somerset scored 355 for the loss of one wicket, Jerry's contribution being 234 – surely some sort of record. At the end of the season Jerry was capped, a deserved reward for his tenacity in getting into the county game.

Somerset did not sign him up full time until 1980 when he had reached the ripe old age of 26. Yet he had played regularly in youth sides and second XI matches in 1974 and '75. He gave up a career in banking to go on the Lord's groundstaff for two years and had trials elsewhere before Somerset eventually relented and offered the full-time contract that they must have debated in 1975. Having watched Jerry play at school from the age of ten upwards, I'd always been surprised by the club's reluctance to snap him up.

Perhaps they thought him too chancy or too casual at the wicket. However, since he's been introduced to first team cricket he has tightened up his technique and on his day is the most effortless timer of a cricket ball. His off-spinners, it is embarrassing to relate, have a tendency to spin more than mine. In 1982 we were the only recognised spinners in the club and so we often found ourselves bowling in tandem, an experience we first shared in 1966. However, I doubt whether we'll be doing the same thing in another sixteen years.

At Lord's, Somerset's second home. Nottingham are the victims. (Somerset County Gazette).

11. 1983

The 1983 season was disjointed for several reasons: the World Cup deprived us of four players; Brian Rose missed the last three months because of a mysterious back injury and Hallam Moseley's shoulder prevented him from playing at all. Throughout the year we had four captains – Rose, Botham, Richards and Roebuck – all effective in their contrasting styles but inevitably posing problems through the lack of continuity. We rarely played the same side for two games in succession.

At least the situation allowed Peter Robinson, the club coach, to introduce some of his youngsters to first class cricket, and all of them showed distinct possibilities for the future. From Keynsham came Richard Ollis and Julian Wyatt, one a punchy left hander, the other a calm, economical opening batsman. Nigel Felton, another Millfield product, scored 170 against his former employers, Kent, no doubt causing a few eyebrows to be raised in the committee rooms at Canterbury. Mark Davies, a left arm medium pace bowler from Kilve, surprised several established opening batsmen with his nippy inswingers. Gary Palmer, son of Ken, who had made his debut in 1982 at the tender age of 16, refused to be overawed by any adversary. Indeed when a player of the stature of Dennis Amiss made his way to the wicket he was liable to ask, 'Who's this bloke, then?' To augment these home-grown players we recruited Hugh Wilson from Surrey and Steven Booth from Yorkshire. It was refreshing to see some new faces in the dressing room after six years of little change.

The improvements carried out at the county ground over the last four years were rewarded when Taunton was chosen as a venue for the 1983 World Cup. Gordon Prosser, who had succeeded Don Price and Cecil Buttle in the vital role of head groundsman, ensured that the county ground was in immaculate condition. Five perfect practice wickets were prepared for the visiting teams, the stands were spotless and they even painted the covers.

England played Sri Lanka and it proved to be a grand occasion. A good humoured crowd filled the stands and enjoyed a feast of runs on a perfect batting pitch. Their only disappointment was when Ian Botham, who had relished the prospect of playing for England on his home ground, was run out without scoring. England won comfortably but not before several of the Sri Lankans had discovered some of the advantages of batting with such short, straight boundaries. Everyone was impressed by the club's handling of the fixture and it was whispered, 'Maybe a Test match next time?'

Meanwhile at Bath a Somerset side lacking six regulars defeated Glamorgan in the John Player League thanks to a fine team performance brilliantly orchestrated by our captain, Peter Roebuck. The newcomers to the side relished their new-found responsibility and paved the way for another assault upon the John Player League title. Yet again we were to finish second, a downpour at Chelmsford on the last Sunday of the season providing Yorkshire with a coveted trophy after their years in the wilderness. Our record in the John Player League over the last ten years has been remarkable. We won the trophy in 1979 and have been second no less than six times.

However the Nat West competition provided the greatest excitement. After eliminating Shropshire in the first round we visited Old Trafford. On a crumbling surface, unsuitable for one-day cricket, Lancashire were restricted to 163 for 6. When Somerset were 66 for 2, with Richards gone, the match was in the balance. Not for the first time Peter Roebuck and Nigel Popplewell guided us to victory, Nigel scoring 68 not out in a partnership of 98. The match was televised and, when Somerset's number four strode out to the wicket, Jim Laker, commenting for the BBC, announced, 'You can tell it's Popplewell by the colour of his boots.'

Until very recently Nigel has not been noted for his sartorial elegance on the cricket field. He was introduced to Somerset by Pete Roebuck, his contemporary at Cambridge. Initially he had an unnecessarily low opinion of himself: he'd declare that he was just a 'bits and pieces man – a poor man's Botham, even a poor man's Marks.' Gradually he has proved to himself and everyone else that he can dominate games in his own right. Now he positively relishes batting under pressure: the right hand slips further down the handle and he waits for the ball to crash square on the off side or 'lap' to the square leg

Nigel Popplewell with Roy Kerslake – a picture of sartorial elegance – off the field. (Somerset County Gazette).

Nigel receives his cap from Brian Rose. (Somerset County Gazette).

Trevor Gard seems highly delighted at winning the Player of the Year Award, 1983. (Somerset County Gazette).

Gary Palmer (Somerset County Gazette).

Hugh Wilson. (Somerset County Gazette).

Julian Wyatt. (Somerset County Gazette).

Mark Davis. (Somerset County Gazette).

Trevor Gard, who is equally adept at keeping ferrets.
(Somerset County Gazette).

Nigel Popplewell – the right hand grips the bat tighter in tense situations. (Somerset County Gazette).

England v Sri Lanka, June, 1983. England comes to Taunton. I give Mike Gatting some practice. (Somerset County Gazette).

boundary. His record during the 1983 cup run underlines his ability to rise to the occasion.

When he decides to disregard every single page of the MCC coaching manual the effect can be devastating. At Bath against Gloucestershire he scored a century in 41 minutes. Unfortunately I missed the innings but I'm assured that the Gloucestershire bowlers were not simply feeding him runs to hasten the declaration; those despatched into the sponsor's tents included such battle-hardened professionals as John Shepherd and David Graveney. Imagine his disgust when his fastest century of the year was surpassed on the last day of the season by Steve O'Shaughnessy of Lancashire who made the most of a succession of full tosses from the Leicestershire bowlers.

Nigel is a brilliant catcher, whether diving in the deep or crouched at forward short leg. His birthday is 8th August, and each year my conscience pricks me and I splash out on a pair of shin pads for him. I've yet to find a pair big enough. Nonetheless he takes the knocks as well as the catches with an infectious grin and has never yet expressed the desire to seek certain revenge – by having me posted to forward short leg when he's bowling.

He is an effervescent personality on and off the field and most of the time he manages very successfully to disguise the fact that he is a Cambridge graduate. After a game he can often be spotted with a pint in his hand and a 'Wurzel' song in his throat (despite coming from Buckinghamshire). Perhaps he saves his academic powers for the winter when he seeks out a tie and a smart jacket and sets about educating the pupils of Taunton School. I imagine that his lessons are well worth attending.

In the next round we travelled to Hove, where Sussex were bundled out for 65 as Garner (4–8) and Botham (4–20) ran riot. Arthur Milton, the match adjudicator, displayed wonderful West Country logic after the game. He announced that it had been impossible for him to separate the performances of Botham and Garner so he had decided to give the Man of the Match award to Trevor Gard, who had taken five superb catches behind the stumps. It was a popular choice.

Team photograph taken before the Nat West quarter final against Sussex at Hove. There were more smiles after the game. Standing (from left to right): G. V. Palmer, N. F. M. Popplewell, J. W. Lloyds, C. H. Dredge, P. M. Roebuck, R. L. Ollis, T. Gard, P. A. Slocombe. seated (from left to right): J. Garner, I. V. A Richards, I. T. Botham, P. W. Denning, V. J. Marks. (Somerset County Gazette).

Trevor had waited almost ten years to become the side's first-choice wicket keeper, yet he never resented the continued presence of Derek Taylor, choosing instead to pick his predecessor's brains and to improve his technique. He admitted to being very nervous at the prospect of his first full season in county cricket but no one could have detected any sign of this. At the beginning of May he pottered out onto the ground sweaterless, with his cap perched on top of his head as if he were fetching the morning newspaper: he might have been a regular member of the side for fifteen years.

He has many similarities to his predecessor: he is not an eye-catching keeper, preferring to go about his business with quiet efficiency rather than unnecessary flourishes. If anything his appealing is even more high-pitched than Derek's; I am sure stray dogs can hear him but whether umpires do is highly debatable. He is also very reticent behind the stumps compared with some of his colleagues on the county circuit. Whenever I ask him why he hasn't supported one of my desperate appeals for lbw he quietly informs me that the ball was missing the leg stump by at least an inch.

Nor is his batting dissimilar to Derek's: he positively enjoys blocking. Admittedly, when long hops and full tosses come his way he tries to whack them, but always with an air of reluctance. Occasionally he'll have 'half a do' which might, if the shot is perfectly timed, send the ball over the infield. Perhaps I do him an injustice. He has a sound technique and will score valuable runs in Somerset's last middle order in the years to come; at Heanor in 1938 he hit his first six, as he was quick to point out on our way back to the

Nigel Popplewell square cuts. (Somerset County Gazette).

Pete Denning, the injured Rose and I slump on a bench after the Nat West Final against Kent in 1983. (Somerset County Gazette).

hotel. He has inherited the role of nightwatchman and he sets about that task with the grim determination of one of Captain Mainwaring's privates.

His earthy common sense made him an obvious choice when selecting Somerset's representative at the Cricketers' Association but he's hardly an Arthur Scargill figure. He has quickly become a favourite with the crowd as they can easily recognise him for what he is – a gentle Somerset man from West Lambrook, who enjoys the pleasures of the countryside. As well as keeping wicket he's a dab hand at keeping ferrets and he's happiest roaming the hills with his ferret or his twelve-bore, stemming the damage to the fruit and vegetable farm on which he works in the winter.

The semi-final was at Lord's on 17th August, against Middlesex, the Championships leaders who had already won the Benson & Hedges competition. Sent into bat by Botham, they scored 222 for 9 off their 55 overs, thanks to robust efforts from Slack, Gatting and Tomlins. In reply Somerset collapsed to 52 for 5 against the pace of Norman Cowans and Neil Williams. The situation looked desperate, our only consolation being that we had packed our side with batting, with Popplewell at number seven and – dare I say it? – Marks at number eight.

Botham and Popplewell decided to occupy the crease, attempting nothing extravagant. However, when Emburey was introduced, Botham heaved him into the Mound stand and he was immediately withdrawn from the attack. Thereafter Gatting decided to defend when Botham was facing, and to attack Popplewell. Nigel, however, was unmoved by the cluster of close fieldsmen and withstood the guiles of Edmonds and the speed of Daniel and Cowans. As Ian picked up singles Nigel occasionally unleashed his square drive down to the Tavern, and the partnership gradually gained momentum. The hundred partnership had just been recorded, when

Ian Botham played with great self-discipline in the semi final against Middlesex, 1983. (Somerset County Gazette).

Nat West v Kent, 1983. Somerset win by 24 runs and the fans invade the pitch. (Somerset County Gazette).

A wicket falls in the Nat West Final. Umpire D. Constant keeps his index finger warm. (Somerset County Gazette).

Somerset v Middlesex, Nat West Trophy Semi-Final
17th August, 1983

MIDDLESEX	
G. D. Barlow, c Botham b Garner	8
W. N. Slack, c Slocombe b Popplewell	57
C. T. Radley, b Marks	12
*M. W. Gatting, c Marks b Popplewell	49
K. P. Tomlins, c Botham b Garner	58
J. E. Emburey, c Marks b Popplewell	1
†P. R. Downton, b Garner	12
N. F. Williams, lbw b Botham	2
P. H. Edmonds, not out	7
W. W. Daniel, run out	0
N. G. Cowans, not out	0
Extras (l-b 11, w 5)	16
9 wickets	222

Fall of wickets: 1/16, 2/55, 3/117, 4/148, 5/163, 6/204, 7/211, 8/213, 9/215.

Bowling: Garner 11–3–23–3; Botham 12–2–33–1; Dredge 9–0–48–0; Richards 12–3–23–0; Marks 8–0–45–1; Popplewell 8–0–34–3.

SOMERSET	
P. M. Roebuck, c Gatting b Cowans	7
J. W. Lloyds, c Downton b Cowans	7
P. W. Denning, b Cowans	0
I. V. A. Richards, c Daniel b Williams	23
P. A. Slocombe, c Downton b Williams	2
*I. T. Botham, not out	96
N. F. M. Popplewell, c Downton b Daniel	46
V. J. Marks, c Emburey b Slack	21
J. Garner, run out	0
†T. Gard, not out	0
C. H. Dredge,	
Extras (l-b 6, w 4, n-b 10)	20
8 wickets	222

Fall of wickets: 1/13, 2/13, 3/41, 4/43, 5/52, 6/156, 7/218, 8/221.

Bowling: Daniel 12–2–32–1; Cowans 12–2–48–3; Williams 12–0–54–2; Emburey 3–1—9–0; Edmonds 12–4–33–0; Slack 9–1–26–1.

Somerset won on a tie with fewer wickets lost

Somerset spectators celebrate winning the Nat West Trophy,
1983. (Somerset County Gazette).

Nat West Final v Kent, the two captains in action, Botham
and Chris Tavaré. (Somerset County Gazette).

Nigel flashed once too often at Daniel and his typically gutsy innings of 46 was over.

In a sense I was relieved to get to the wicket as I'd been pacing up and down the dressing room for almost two hours. I'd long since exhausted my repertoire of practice strokes and from my viewpoint the Middlesex bowling had looked incredibly menacing. Once in the middle the nerves started to evaporate and the realisation came that it was quite possible to win a game that had seemed beyond redemption at tea time. In tight situations it is infinitely preferable to be at the crease rather than watching as a helpless spectator in the pavilion.

In fading light the Middlesex side were becoming desperate as Ian started to open his shoulders for the final assault. We only had to stay together to win the game and their strike bowlers were running out of overs. With just five needed off two overs I holed out to deep square leg off Wilf Slack. Even as the ball was dropping into the hands of Emburey the Botham brain was still functioning smoothly: he yelled at me to cross so that he could retain the strike. In the same over Joel was run out. At the start of the final over of the game the scores were level and Ian was 96 not out. After several minutes of consultation amongst the Middlesex players, the batsmen and the umpires, Emburey was summoned to bowl. We required one run to be certain of victory; Middlesex required two wickets. Ian had ensured that he had the strike and, despite the fact that he had a glorious century within his grasp, he proceeded to block the last six balls of the match with exaggerated care. Somerset had won because they had lost fewer wickets. Botham's innings, characterised by its self discipline and control rather than by his normal ferocious hitting, inevitably ensured him the Man of the Match award. All engagements for 3rd September were cancelled.

Nat West Final at Lord's v Kent, 1983. Wilson, Denning, Lloyds and Felton view the action on television. Botham in the corner watches live. (Somerset County Gazette).

Ian Botham's turn to loft the Nat West Trophy. Graham
Johnson is not impressed. (Bristol United Press).

Nigel Popplewell is regarded as a bottom handed player – and you can see why. Nat West Final v Kent, 1983. (Somerset County Gazette).

Trevor's brilliant stumping of Aslett off Viv Richards. Nat West Final, 1983. (Somerset County Gazette).

So we end where we started, at a Lord's final in September between Somerset and Kent. Again the Kent balcony is garlanded with hops and the Somerset supporters gather in the Tavern with barrels of cider over their shoulders. Two members of the Kent side, Derek Underwood and Alan Knott, have survived the intervening years, but Colin Cowdrey has now been replaced by his son, Chris; for the sake of symmetry it is a pity that Gary Palmer hasn't forced himself into the Somerset team in succession to Ken. However this time the roles are reversed. Despite the presence of Knott and Underwood and a powerful combination of promising young players, Kent are regarded as the underdogs. Somerset, with seven of the side having four Cup final appearances behind them, are expected to win. This time the butterflies are more active in the Kent dressing room.

The game followed a similar pattern to the 1967 Cup final. Bad light prevented a prompt start and the match was sensibly reduced to 50 overs per side by umpires David Constant and David Evans. Chris Tavare won the toss and invited us to bat. Graham Dilley, anxious to claim a touring place for the winter, began with a hostile opening spell, removing our openers Denning and Roebuck in his first five overs. Phil Slocombe, promoted in the order, and Viv Richards, then staged a recovery adding 69, but both were dismissed just before lunch. Afterwards neither Ian nor Jerry Lloyds was able to break loose, and it was left to Nigel and myself to indulge in the final onslaught. Modesty does not quite forbid me mentioning a six I walloped off Cowdrey in the final over, up into the seats I'd occupied sixteen years before. Our final score of 193 was exactly the same as Kent's winning total in 1967.

A strange feature of the semi-final and the final was that the two best spin bowlers in the world bowled only three overs between them. Underwood wasn't required at all. Initially this was probably because of the presence of Richards, the only batsman I've seen who has consistently mastered Derek's perfect control of line and length, and after Viv's dismissal the seam bowlers maintained their stranglehold almost to the end. Nevertheless several of us were extremely relieved that we didn't have to face him.

Popplewell, caught Cowdrey, bowled Dilley for 35. Nat West Final, 1983. (Somerset County Gazette).

Botham and Marks posing with Somerset's best bowler before the England v Sri Lanka World Cup Match. (Somerset County Gazette).

Joel gave us the perfect start, having Mark Benson snapped up at first slip by Jerry Lloyds, but Graham Johnson and Chris Tavaré stood firm until the tea interval when the Kent total had reached 46 for 1 off 14 overs. Over the ham sandwiches we decided to try our slower bowlers, Viv's assortment of seamers and my off spin, in an effort to halt this dangerous partnership.

Chris Tavaré, my contemporary at Oxford, had watched me when I first started bowling seriously and was more aware than most of my limitations. After tea it was immediately apparent that he had decided to attack my off spinners, no doubt mindful of his university days when he had regularly deposited them into the undergrowth of the Parks. He stepped away to leg to make room for his cover drive and then advanced down the wicket to smash me over mid on. Graham Johnson, trying to emulate his captain, lifted his head and was bowled. However, I could sense that Chris was undeterred by his partner's dismissal: after a few years' experience spinners can usually gauge when a batsman is full of aggressive

intent. In my fifth over, even though the field was deep set, he came down the wicket and drove the ball sweetly straight into the safe hands of Pete Roebuck at deep mid wicket.

Chris, despite his Test match reputation, was the lynchpin of Kent's one-day side: with him gone Kent were on the defensive. In the same over Trevor Gard executed a brilliant legside stumping off a slower off break and we had begun to take control of the match. At the other end Viv was bowling beautifully. Over the last couple of years Viv has developed into an excellent medium pacer, despite his apparently casual attitude to bowling. With the score at 89 Trevor produced another quicksilver piece of wicketkeeping to stump Derek Aslett off Richards.

Thereafter the Kent batsmen flailed away in a manner reminiscent of Graham Burgess in 1967, more in hope than expectation. Graham Dilley smashed sixteen off one over but Botham returned to bowl him. Garner ended Ellison's stout resistance and when Kevin Jarvis scooped Colin Dredge to midwicket the match was over. The winning margin was 24 runs as opposed to 32 in 1967.

Afterwards our players reacted to our victory true to form. Popplewell was irrepressible, Botham soaked

Nat West v Kent, 1983. Ian Botham pulls Cowdrey ...
(Somerset County Gazette).

Somerset v Kent, Nat West Trophy Final
3rd September, 1983

The match was reduced to 50 overs per side

SOMERSET

P. W. Denning, lbw b Dilley	1
P. M. Roebuck, b Dilley	11
P. A. Slocombe, c Johnson b Baptiste	20
I. V. A. Richards, c Knott b Dilley	51
*I. T. Botham, c Johnson b Cowdrey	9
N. F. M. Popplewell, c Cowdrey b Dilley	35
J. W. Lloyds, lbw b Jarvis	10
V. J. Marks, c Benson b Cowdrey	29
J. Garner, run out	4
C. H. Dredge, not out	3
†T. Gard,	
Extras (b 1, w 2, n-b 17)	20
9 wickets	**193**

Fall of wickets: 1/10, 2/20, 3/89, 4/95, 5/112, 6/146,
7/176, 8/190, 9/193.
Bowling: Dilley 10–1–29–4; Ellison 10–1–35–0;
Jarvis 10–0–43–1; Baptiste 10–1–37–1; Cowdrey 10–2–29–2.

KENT

M. R. Benson, c Lloyds b Garner	0
G. W. Johnson, b Marks	27
*C. J. Tavaré, c Roebuck b Marks	39
D. G. Aslett, st Gard b Richards	14
C. S. Cowdrey, st Gard b Marks	0
E. A. Baptiste, b Botham	16
†A. P. E. Knott, c Roebuck b Dredge	17
R. M. Ellison, b Garner	21
G. R. Dilley, b Botham	19
D. L. Underwood, not out	5
K. B. S. Jarvis, c Botham b Dredge	3
Extras (b 6, l-b 1, n-b 1)	8
47.1 overs	**169**

Fall of wickets: 1/0, 2/60, 3/73, 4/73, 5/88, 6/112,
7/126, 8/160, 9/162.
Bowling: Garner 9–2–15–2; Botham 10–0–29–2;
Dredge 8.1–0–50–2; Popplewell 1–0–9–0;
Marks 10–0–30–3; Richards 9–1–28–1.

Somerset won by 24 runs

all comers in champagne. Dasher and I slumped
on a bench gathering our thoughts. Trevor Gard,
making a Cup final appearance in his first season,
was watery-eyed. It seemed fitting that he should
keep the ball as a souvenir of his inspired wicketkeeping.

. . . and is caught by Johnson. (Somerset County Gazette).

Somerset's reputation as lovable losers has now been buried for a while. Over the last five years, five trophies have been won and our expertise in the one-day game has been universally acknowledged. The county ground has been modernised and the club treasurer, although still harassed, is not constantly on the verge of a mental breakdown. Our older supporters must be rather bewildered by the sudden change in fortunes. However, the greatest challenge for professional cricketers, the winning of the Championship, still remains. If we can muster the consistency to win that title then there will be cause for celebrations on a grand scale, and someone somewhere will be forced to share a drink with Sammy Woods in honour of Somerset County Cricket Club.

Ian Botham listening to Club Chairman, Michael Hill.
(Somerset County Gazette).

Trevor Gard on tiptoe. (Somerset County Gazette).

Somerset v Warwickshire, John Player League, 1983, at
Taunton. Botham about to be caught at long off. (Somerset
County Gazette).

REFERENCES

1. Robertson-Glasgow, R. C., *46 Not Out*, Hollis & Carter, 1948, pp 153–154
2. Foot, David, *From Grace to Botham*, Redcliffe Press, Bristol, 1980, p 88.
3. Andrews, Bill, *The Hand that Bowled Bradman*, Macdonald, 1973, p 79.
4. Roebuck, Peter, *Slices of Cricket*, Allen & Unwin, 1982, pp 46, 71, 79, 122, 127.
5. Alley, Bill, *My Incredible Innings*, Pelham Books, 1969, p 84.
6. *Up From Somerset for the Cup*, edited & published by John Davies, 23A North Road, Bristol 6, for and on behalf of the Somerset Players Welfare Fund, 1967. Quotations from contributions by Colin Atkinson, Brian Statham.
7. *Wisden Cricketers' Almanack*, Sporting Handbooks, 1968, p 669.
8. Arlott, John, writing in the benefit brochure for Mervyn Kitchen's benefit year, 1973.
9. Close, Brian, *I Don't Bruise Easily*, Macdonald & Jane, in association with Futura Publications, 1978, pp 142, 207, 233, 222.
10. *Wisden Cricketers' Almanack*, Sporting Handbooks, 1973, p 393.
11. Richards, Vivian, with Foot, David, *Viv Richards*, World's Work, 1979, Quotations taken from W. H. Allen Star Books paperback edition, 1982, pp 9, 113.
12. Hill, Eric, writing in *Somerset Cricket Handbook*, Somerset County Cricket Club, 1983.
13. Gibson, Alan, writing in the benefit brochure for Peter Denning's benefit year, 1981.
14. *Wisden Cricketers' Almanack*, Queen Anne Press, 1978, p 660.
15. Woodcock, John, writing in *The Times*, Saturday, 2nd September, 1978.
16. Rose, Brian, 'Captain's Column', the *Somerset County Gazette*, 1979, 1980.